NPCA National Park Guide Series

NATIONAL PARKS AND CONSERVATION ASSOCIATION

GUIDE TO NATIONAL PARKS
SOUTHEAST REGION

Written and compiled by Russell D. Butcher for the National Parks and
Conservation Association and edited by Lynn P. Whitaker

NPCA is America's only private, nonprofit citizen organization dedicated solely
to protecting, preserving, and enhancing the U.S. National Park System. The
association's mission is to protect and enhance America's National Park System
for present and future generations.

The
Globe
Pequot
Press

Guilford, Connecticut

Photo credits: pages i, 7, 11, 34–35, 37, 47, 69 © Tom Till; pages iv–v, 15, 21, 24–25, 45, 50–51 © Laurence Parent; page iii © Willard Clay; pages viii, 12, 27, 30 © Jeff Foott; page 42 © Carr Clifton; pages 53, 56 © William Neill/Larry Ulrich Stock; page 59 © John Elk III; page 63 © Larry Ulrich.

Maps: © Trails Illustrated, a division of National Geographic Maps
Cover design and text design: Adam Schwartzman
Cover photo: Natchez Trace Parkway, Mississippi (© Laurence Parent)

Library of Congress Cataloging-in-Publication Data

Butcher, Russell D.
    National parks and conservation association guide to national parks: Southeast region / written and compiled by Russell D. Butcher for the National Parks and Conservation Association. ; and edited by Lynn P. Whitaker. —1st ed.
       p.   cm. — (NPCA national park guide series)
    ISBN 0-7627-0576-0
    1. Southern States Guidebooks. 2. National parks and preserves—Southern States Guidebooks. I. Whitaker, Lynn P. II. National Parks and Conservation Association. III. Title. IV. Series.
F207.3.B88 1999
917.504'43—DC21

99–15690
CIP

♻ Printed on recycled paper
Printed and bound in Quebec, Canada
First edition/First printing

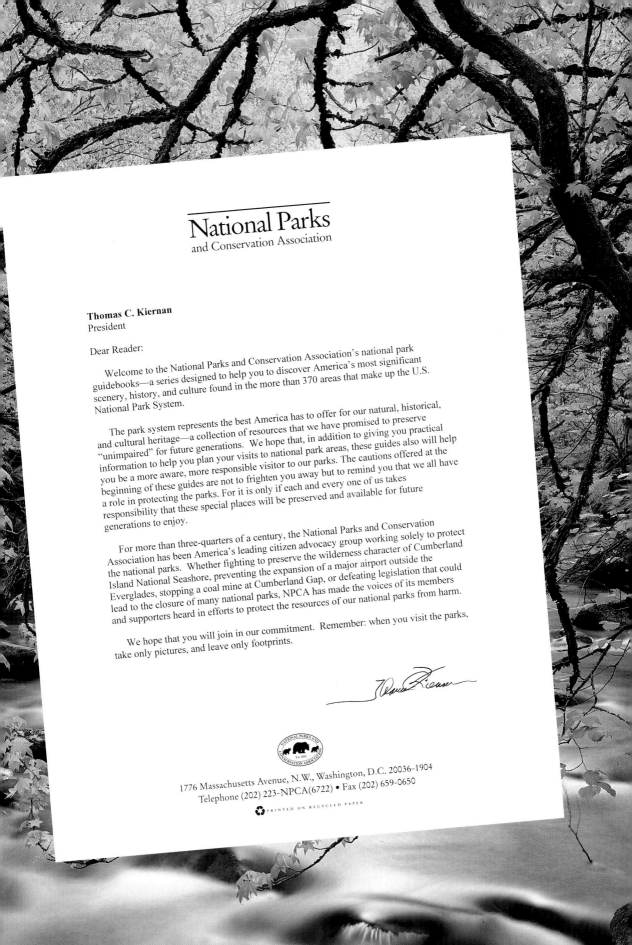

National Parks
and Conservation Association

Thomas C. Kiernan
President

Dear Reader:

Welcome to the National Parks and Conservation Association's national park guidebooks—a series designed to help you to discover America's most significant scenery, history, and culture found in the more than 370 areas that make up the U.S. National Park System.

The park system represents the best America has to offer for our natural, historical, and cultural heritage—a collection of resources that we have promised to preserve "unimpaired" for future generations. We hope that, in addition to giving you practical information to help you plan your visits to national park areas, these guides also will help you be a more aware, more responsible visitor to our parks. The cautions offered at the beginning of these guides are not to frighten you away but to remind you that we all have a role in protecting the parks. For it is only if each and every one of us takes responsibility that these special places will be preserved and available for future generations to enjoy.

For more than three-quarters of a century, the National Parks and Conservation Association has been America's leading citizen advocacy group working solely to protect the national parks. Whether fighting to preserve the wilderness character of Cumberland Island National Seashore, preventing the expansion of a major airport outside the Everglades, stopping a coal mine at Cumberland Gap, or defeating legislation that could lead to the closure of many national parks, NPCA has made the voices of its members and supporters heard in efforts to protect the resources of our national parks from harm.

We hope that you will join in our commitment. Remember: when you visit the parks, take only pictures, and leave only footprints.

1776 Massachusetts Avenue, N.W., Washington, D.C. 20036-1904
Telephone (202) 223-NPCA(6722) • Fax (202) 659-0650
PRINTED ON RECYCLED PAPER

CONTENTS

7
11
15
21
27
37
47
53
59
63
69

Southeast Region

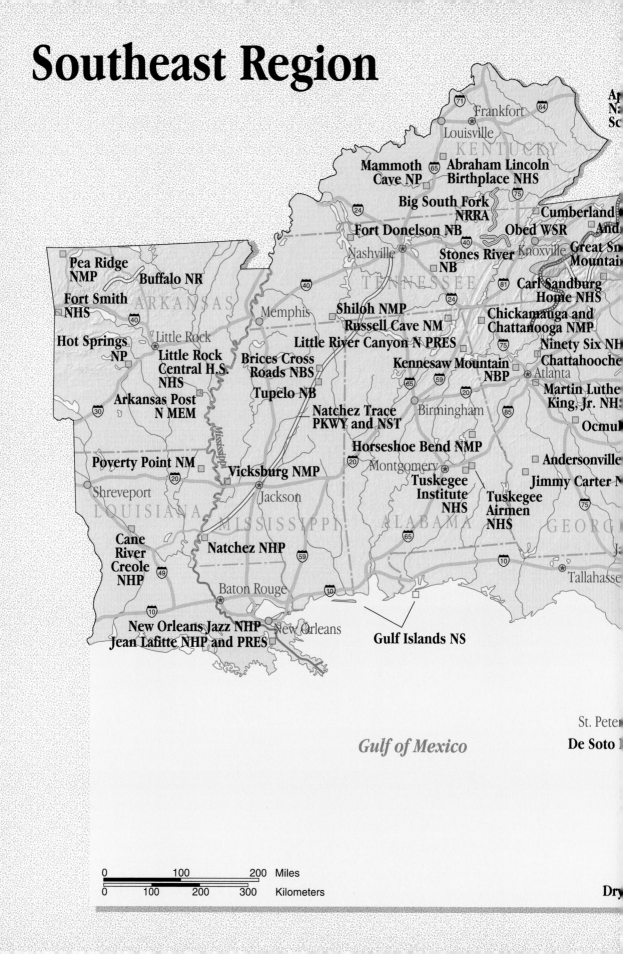

Frankfort

Louisville

KENTUCKY

Mammoth Cave NP

Abraham Lincoln Birthplace NHS

Big South Fork NRRA

Cumberland
An

Fort Donelson NB

Obed WSR

Nashville

Knoxville

Great Sm
Mountai

Stones River NB

TENNESSEE

Carl Sandburg Home NHS

Pea Ridge NMP

Buffalo NR

ARKANSAS

Memphis

Shiloh NMP

Russell Cave NM

Chickamauga and Chattanooga NMP

Fort Smith NHS

Little River Canyon N PRES

Ninety Six NH

Chattahooche

Hot Springs NP

Little Rock

Little Rock Central H.S. NHS

Brices Cross Roads NBS

Kennesaw Mountain NBP

Atlanta

Tupelo NB

Martin Luthe King, Jr. NH

Arkansas Post N MEM

Natchez Trace PKWY and NST

Birmingham

Ocmul

Horseshoe Bend NMP

Poverty Point NM

Vicksburg NMP

Montgomery

Andersonville

LOUISIANA

Jackson

MISSISSIPPI

ALABAMA

Tuskegee Institute NHS

Jimmy Carter N

Tuskegee Airmen NHS

GEORG

Cane River Creole NHP

Natchez NHP

Shreveport

Baton Rouge

Tallahasse

New Orleans Jazz NHP

Jean Lafitte NHP and PRES

New Orleans

Gulf Islands NS

St. Peter

De Soto

Gulf of Mexico

Dry

| 0 | 100 | 200 | Miles |
| 0 | 100 | 200 | 300 | Kilometers |

ian

ail

lue Ridge
KWY

**Wright Brothers
N MEM**

Guilford Courthouse NMP

Fort Raleigh NHS

P

nson NHS   Raleigh ✦

NORTH
CAROLINA

Cape Hatteras NS

Charlotte

Kings Mountain NMP

pens NB

Cape Lookout NS

SOUTH

AROLINA

Moores Creek NB

Columbia

r NRA

Congaree Swamp NM

Charleston

M

**Charles Pinckney NHS
Fort Sumter NM**

Atlantic

Ocean

Fort Pulaski NM

Fort Frederica NM

Cumberland Island NS

ville **Timucuan Ecological and Historic Preserve**

Fort Caroline N MEM

Castillo de San Marcos NM

Fort Matanzas NM

Canaveral NS

Tampa

FLORIDA

*Lake
Okeechobee*

ypress
N PRES

Miami

**Biscayne
NP**

**Everglades
NP**

gas NP

Puerto Rico
San Juan
San Juan NHS

Virgin Islands
Virgin Islands NP

Charlotte Amalie
Buck Island Reef NM

**Salt River Bay NHP
and Ecological Preserve**   **Christiansted NHS**

▲ Fort Pickens, Gulf Islands National Seashore, Florida

GENERAL INFORMATION

Whether you're an American history buff or a birdwatcher, a lover of rocky coastlines or marshy swamps, a dedicated environmentalist or a weekend rambler, and whether you're seeking a way to spend a carefully planned month-long vacation or an unexpectedly free sunny afternoon—the national parks are for you. They offer a broad spectrum of natural and cultural resources in all 50 states as well as Guam, Puerto Rico, the Virgin Islands, and American Samoa where you can learn, exercise, participate in activities, and be constantly moved and inspired by the riches available. Perhaps most important of all, as one of the National Park System's 280 million annual visitors, you become part of the attempt to preserve our natural and historical treasures for present and future generations.

This guidebook will help you do that, as one in a series of eight Regional National Park Guides covering all the units in the National Park System. This section of general information provides both an overview of key facts that can be applied to every unit and a brief history of the National Parks and Conservation Association.

SPECIAL PARK PASSES

Some parks charge entrance fees to help offset their operational costs. Several options for special entrance passes are available, enabling you to choose the most appropriate and economical way for you and your family and friends to visit sites.

Park Pass: For this annual entrance permit to a specific fee-charging park, monument, historic site, or recreation area in the National Park System, the cost is usually $10 or $15 depending on the area. Such a pass does not cover any fees other than entrance for permit holder and any accompanying passengers in a private noncommercial vehicle or, in the case of walk-in facilities, the permit holder's spouse,

children, and parents. The pass may be purchased in person or by mail from the unit at which it will be used. It is nontransferable and nonrefundable.

Golden Eagle Passport: This annual entrance pass admits visitors to all the federal lands that charge entrance fees; these include national parks, monuments, historic sites, recreation areas, national forests, and national wildlife refuges. The pass costs $50 and is valid for one year from purchase. It does not cover any fees other than entrance for permit holder and any accompanying passengers in a private noncommercial vehicle or, in the case of walk-in facilities, the holder's spouse, children, and parents. The Golden Eagle Passport may be purchased in person or by mail from the National Park Service, Office of Public Inquiries, Room 1013, U.S. Department of the Interior, 18th & C Streets, N.W., Washington, DC 20240 (202-208-4747) or at any of the seven National Park Service field offices, any of the nine U.S. Forest Service regional offices, or any national park unit and other federal areas that charge an entrance fee. It is nontransferable and nonrefundable.

Golden Age Passport: A one-time $10 fee for this pass allows lifetime entrance to all federal fee-charging areas as described in the Golden Eagle Passport section for citizens and permanent residents of the United States who are 62 years of age or older and any accompanying passengers in a private noncommercial vehicle or, in the case of walk-in facilities, the holder's spouse and children. This pass also entitles the holder to a 50 percent discount on use fees charged in park areas. The Golden Age Passport must be obtained IN PERSON at any of the locations listed in the Golden Eagle Passport section; mail requests are not accepted. Applicants must provide proof of age, such as a driver's license or birth certificate, or sign an affidavit attesting to eligibility.

Golden Access Passport: This free lifetime entrance permit to all federal fee-charging areas as described in the Golden Eagle Passport section is available for citizens and permanent residents of the United States who are visually impaired or permanently disabled and any accompanying passengers in a private noncommercial vehicle or, in the case of walk-in facilities, the permit holder's spouse, children, and parents. It also entitles the holder to a 50 percent discount on use fees charged in park areas. The Golden Access Passport must be obtained IN PERSON at any of the locations listed in the Golden Eagle Passport section; mail requests are not accepted. Applicant must provide proof of eligibility to receive federal benefits or sign an affidavit attesting to one's eligibility.

PASSPORT TO YOUR NATIONAL PARKS

The *Passport to Your National Parks* is a special commemorative item designed to serve as a companion for park visitors. This informative and unique publication records each visit through special regional and national stamps and cancellations. When you visit any national park, be sure to have your Passport canceled with a rubber stamp marking the name of the park and the date you were there. The Passport gives you the opportunity to share and relive your journey through America's national parks and will become a travel record to cherish for years. Passports cost $4.95; a full set of ten national and regional stamps is $3.95. The national parks represented in the stamp set vary from year to year. For ordering information, call 800-821-2903, or write to Eastern National Park & Monument Association, 110 Hector Street, Suite 105, Conshohocken, PA 19428.

HELPFUL TRIP-PLANNING PUBLICATIONS

Two volumes offer descriptive text on the National Park System: *Exploring Our National Parks and Monuments,* by Devereux Butcher (ninth edition by Russell D. Butcher), and *Exploring Our National Historic Parks and Sites,* by Russell D. Butcher. These books feature descriptions and black-and-white photographs of more than 370 National Park System units. Both volumes also contain chap-

ters on possible new parks, threats to the parks, a history of NPCA, and the national park standards. To order, contact Roberts Rinehart Publishers, 6309 Monarch Park Place, Niwot, CO 80503; 800-352-1985 or 303-530-4400.

NPCA offers the following brochures at no charge: *The National Parks: How to Have a Quality Experience* and *Visiting Battlefields: The Civil War.* These brochures provide helpful information on how best to enjoy a visit to the national parks. NPCA members can also receive the *Park System Map and Guide, The National Parks Index, The National Parks Camping Guide,* and *Lesser Known Areas* as part of NPCA's PARK-PAK by calling 202-223-6722, ext. 214.

The Story Behind the Scenery ® and *The Continuing Story* ® series are lavishly illustrated books providing informative text and magnificent photographs of the landscapes, flora, and fauna of our national parklands. More than 100 titles on the national parks, historic events, and Indian cultures, as well as an annual national parks calendar, are available. For information, call toll free 800-626-9673, fax to 702-731-9421, or write to KC Publications, 3245 E. Patrick Lane, Suite A, Las Vegas, NV 89120.

The National Parks: Index and *Lesser Known Areas,* both produced by the National Park Service, can be ordered by contacting the Superintendent of Documents, U.S. Government Printing Office, Washington, DC 20402-9325; 202-512-1800. To receive at no charge the *National Park System Map and Guide,* the *National Trails System Map and Guide;* or an *Official Map and Guide* of specific national parks, contact National Park Service, Office of Information, P.O. Box 37127, Washington, DC 20013-7127; 202-208-4747.

National Parks Visitor Facilities and Services is a directory of vendors authorized to serve park visitors through contracts with the National Park Service. Concessionaires offering lodging, food, beverages, outfitting, tours, trail rides, and other activities and services are listed alphabetically. To order, contact the National Park Hospitality Association, 1331

Pennsylvania Ave., N.W., Suite 724, Washington, DC 20004; 202-662-7097.

Great Walks, Inc., publishes six pocket-sized books of detailed information on specific trails in Yosemite; Sequoia and Kings Canyon in California; Big Bend; Great Smoky Mountains; and Acadia and Mount Desert Island in Maine. For information, send $1 (refundable with your first order) to Great Walks, P.O. Box 410, Goffstown, NH 03045.

The U.S. Bureau of Land Management (BLM) offers free maps that detail recreation areas and scenic and backcountry roads and trails. These are available by contacting the BLM at the Department of the Interior, 1849 C St., N.W., Suite 5600, Washington, DC 20240; 202-452-5125. In addition, *Beyond the National Parks: A Recreational Guide to Public Lands in the West,* published by the Smithsonian Institution Press, is an informative guidebook to many special places administered by the BLM. *America's Secret Recreation Areas,* by Michael Hodgson, is an excellent resource for little-known natural areas in 12 Western states. It details 270 million acres of land administered by BLM, with campgrounds, recreational activities, trails, maps, facilities, and much more. The 1995-96 edition is published by Foghorn Press and is available for $17.95 by calling 1-800-FOGHORN.

The National Wildlife Refuge Visitors Guide can be ordered free from the U.S. Fish and Wildlife Service's Publications Unit at 4401 North Fairfax Dr., MS 130 Webb, Arlington, VA 22203; 703-358-1711.

The four-volume *Birds of the National Parks,* by Roland H. Wauer, a retired NPS interpreter and biologist, provides an excellent reference on the parks' birds and their seasons and habitats. This series, written for the average rather than specialist park visitor, is unfortunately out of print.

SAFETY AND REGULATIONS

To protect the national parks' natural and cultural resources and the millions of people who come to enjoy them, the National Park Service asks every visitor to abide by some important regulations. Park staffs do all they can to help you have a safe and pleasant visit, but your cooperation is essential.

Some park hazards—deep lakes, sheer cliffs, extremely hot or cold temperatures—cannot be eliminated. However, accidents and illnesses can be prevented if you use the same common sense you would at home and become familiar with the park. Take some time before your trip or when you first arrive to get to know the park's regulations, warnings, and potential hazards. If you have children, make sure they understand such precautions, and keep a careful watch over them, especially in potentially dangerous situations. If you are injured or become ill, the staff can help by directing you to the nearest medical center and, in some parks, by giving you emergency care.

A few rules and safety tips are common to many parks. At all parks, you must keep your campsite clean and the park free of litter by disposing of refuse in trash receptacles. The National Park Service also asks you to follow federal regulations and refrain from the abuse of alcohol and the use of drugs, which are often contributing factors to injuries and deaths. Other rules and safety tips are outlined in the "Special Advisories and Visitor Ethics" section; more detailed information may be provided in park brochures, on signs, and on bulletin boards at camping areas and other park sites. The National Park Service asks that you report any violation of park regulations to park authorities. If you have any questions, seek the advice of a ranger.

SPECIAL ADVISORIES AND VISITOR ETHICS

Safe Driving

Park roads are designed for sightseeing, not speeding. Because roads are often narrow and winding and sometimes steep, visitors should drive carefully, observe posted speed limits, and be alert for wildlife, pedestrians, bicyclists, other drivers, fallen rocks or trees, slippery roads, and other hazards. Be especially alert for motorists who might stop unexpectedly for sightseeing or wildlife viewing. Visitors are urged to use roadside pullouts instead of stopping on the roadway.

Campfires

Most parks permit fires, as long as certain rules are followed. To avoid a wildfire that would be dangerous to people, property, and natural resources, parks may allow only certain types of campfires—fires only in grills provided, for example, or in designated fire rings. Firewood gathering may be prohibited or restricted to certain areas, so visitors should plan on bringing their own fuel supply. Fires should be kept under control, should never be left unattended, and should be thoroughly extinguished before departure.

Quiet Hours

Out of respect for other visitors, campers should keep noise to a minimum at all times, especially from 10 p.m. to 6 a.m.

Pets

Pets must always be leashed or otherwise physically restrained for the protection of the animal, other visitors, and wildlife. Pets may be prohibited from certain areas, including public buildings, trails, and the backcountry. A few parks prohibit pets altogether. Dog owners are responsible for keeping their pets quiet in camping areas and elsewhere. Guide dogs are exempted from park restrictions. Some parks provide kennel services; contact the park visitor center for information.

Protection of Valuables

Theft is just as much a problem in the national parks as elsewhere, so when leaving a campsite or heading out on a trail, visitors should take valuables along or hide them out of sight in a locked vehicle, preferably in the trunk.

Heat, Cold, and Other Hazards

Visitors should take precautions to deal with the demands and hazards of a park environment. On hot days, pace yourself, schedule strenuous activities for the morning and evening hours, and drink plenty of water and other fluids. On cold days or if you get cold and wet, frostbite and the life-threatening illness called hypothermia can occur, so avoid subjecting yourself to these conditions for long periods. In the thinner air of mountains and high plateaus, even those tasks easy to perform at home can leave one short of breath and dizzy; the best advice is to slow down. If a thunderstorm occurs, avoid exposed areas and open bodies of water, where lightning often strikes, and keep out of low-lying areas and stream beds, where flash floods are most likely to occur.

Wild Plants and Animals

It is the responsibility of every visitor to help preserve the native plants and animals protected in the parks: leave them as you find them, undisturbed and safe. Hunting or carrying a loaded weapon is prohibited in all national parks and national monuments. Hunting during the designated season is allowed in parts of only a few National Park System areas, such as national recreation areas, national preserves, and national seashores and lakeshores. While biting insects or toxic plants, such as poison ivy or poison oak, are the most likely danger you will encounter, visitors should be aware of hazards posed by other wild plants and animals. Rattlesnakes, ticks, and animals carrying rabies or other transmittable diseases, for instance, inhabit some parks. Any wild creature—whether it is as large as a bison or moose or as small as a raccoon or prairie dog—is unpredictable and should be viewed from a distance. Remember that feeding any wild animal is absolutely prohibited.

Campers should especially guard against attracting bears to their campsites as a close encounter with a grizzly, brown, or black bear can result in serious injury or death. Park officials in bear country recommend, and often require, that campers take certain precautions. One is to keep a campsite clean. Bears' sensitive noses can easily detect food left on cans, bottles, and utensils or even personal items with food-like odors (toothpaste, deodorant, etc.). Second, food items should be stored in containers provided by the parks or in your vehicle, preferably out of sight in the trunk.

Bears, especially those in Yosemite, are adept at breaking into cars and other motor vehicles containing even small amounts of food and can cause extensive damage to motor vehicles as they attempt to reach what they can smell. Third, in the backcountry, food should be hung from poles or wires that are provided or from a tree; visitors should inquire at the park as to the recommended placement. In treeless surroundings, campers should store food at least 50 yards from any campsite. If bears inhabit a park on your itinerary, ask the National Park Service for a bear brochure with helpful tips on avoiding trouble in bear country and inquire if bears are a problem where you plan to hike or camp.

Backcountry Camping

Camping in the remote backcountry of a park requires much more preparation than other camping. Most parks require that you pick up a backcountry permit before your trip so that rangers will know about your plans. They can also advise you of hazards and regulations and give you up-to-date information on road, trail, river, lake, or sea conditions, weather forecasts, special fire regulations, availability of water, and other matters. Backcountry permits are available at visitor centers, headquarters, and ranger stations.

There are some basic rules to follow whenever you camp in the backcountry: stay on the trails; pack out all trash; obey fire regulations; be prepared for sudden and drastic weather changes; carry a topographic map or nautical chart when necessary; and carry plenty of food and water. In parks where water is either unavailable or scarce, you may need to carry as much as one gallon of water per person per day. In other parks, springs, streams, or lakes may be abundant, but always purify water before drinking it. Untreated water can carry contaminants. One of the most common, especially in Western parks, is *giardia*, an organism that causes an unpleasant intestinal illness. Water may have to be boiled or purified with tablets; check with the park staff for the most effective treatment.

Sanitation

Visitors should bury human waste six to eight inches below ground and a minimum of 100 feet from a watercourse. Waste water should be disposed of at least 100 feet from a watercourse or campsite. Do not wash yourself, your clothing, or your dishes in any watercourse.

CAMPING RESERVATIONS

Most campsites are available on a first-come, first-served basis, but many sites can be reserved through the National Park Reservation Service. For reservations at Acadia, Assateague Island, Cape Hatteras, Channel Islands, Chickasaw, Death Valley, Everglades, Glacier, Grand Canyon, Great Smoky Mountains, Greenbelt, Gulf Islands, Joshua Tree, Katmai, Mount Rainier, Rocky Mountain, Sequoia-Kings Canyon, Sleeping Bear Dunes, Shenandoah, Whiskeytown, and Zion, call 800-365-CAMP. For reservations for Yosemite National Park, call 800-436-PARK. Reservations can also be made at any of these parks in person. Currently, reservations can be made as much as eight weeks in advance or up to the day before the start of a camping stay. Please have credit card and detailed camping information available when you call in order to facilitate the reservation process.

BIOSPHERE RESERVES AND WORLD HERITAGE SITES

A number of the national park units have received international recognition by the United Nations Educational, Scientific and Cultural Organization for their superlative natural and/or cultural values. Biosphere Reserves are representative examples of diverse natural landscapes, with both a fully protected natural core or park unit and surrounding land being managed to meet human needs. World Heritage Sites include natural and cultural sites with "universal" values that illustrate significant geological processes, may be crucial to the survival of threatened plants and animals, or demonstrate outstanding human achievement.

CHECKLIST FOR HIKING AND CAMPING

Clothing

Rain gear (jacket and pants)
Windbreaker
Parka
Thermal underwear
T-shirt
Long pants and shorts
Extra wool shirt and/or sweater
Hat with brim
Hiking boots
Camp shoes/sneakers
Wool mittens
Lightweight shoes

Equipment

First-aid kit
Pocket knife
Sunglasses
Sunscreen
Topographic map
Compass
Flashlight, fresh batteries, spare bulb
Extra food & water (even for short hikes)
Waterproof matches

Fire starter
Candles
Toilet paper
Digging tool for toilet needs
Day backpack
Sleeping bag
Sleeping pad or air mattress
Tarp/ground sheet
Sturdy tent, preferably free-standing
Insect repellent
Lip balm
Pump-type water filter/water purification
    tablets
Water containers
Plastic trash bags
Biodegradable soap
Small towel
Toothbrush
Lightweight backpack stove/extra fuel
Cooking pot(s)
Eating utensils
Can opener
Electrolyte replacement for plain water (e.g.,
    Gatorade)
Camera, film, lenses, filters
Binoculars
Sewing kit
Lantern
Nylon cord (50 feet)
Whistle
Signal mirror

▲ *Wildflowers, Natchez Trace Parkway, Mississippi*

A BRIEF HISTORY OF THE NATIONAL PARKS AND CONSERVATION ASSOCIATION

In 1916, when Congress established the National Park Service to administer the then nearly 40 national parks and monuments, the agency's first director, Stephen Tyng Mather, quickly saw the need for a private organization, independent of the federal government, to be the citizens' advocate for the parks.

Consequently, on May 19, 1919, the National Parks Association—later renamed the National Parks and Conservation Association (NPCA)—was founded in Washington, D.C. The National Park Service's former public relations director, Robert Sterling Yard, was named to lead the new organization—a position he held for a quarter century.

The association's chief objectives were then and continue to be the following: to vigorously oppose threats to the integrity of the parks; to advocate worthy and consistent standards of *national* significance for the addition of new units to the National Park System; and, through a variety of educational means, to promote the public understanding and appreciation of the parks. From the beginning, threats to the parks have been a major focus of the organization. One of the biggest conservation battles of NPCA's earliest years erupted in 1920, when Montana irrigation interests advocated building a dam and raising the level of Yellowstone Lake in Yellowstone National Park. Fortunately, this threat to the world's first national park was ultimately defeated—the first landmark victory of the fledgling citizens' advocacy group on behalf of the national parks.

At about the same time, a controversy developed over the authority given to the Water Power Commission (later renamed the Federal Power Commission) to authorize the construction of hydropower projects in national parks. The commission had already approved the flooding of Hetch Hetchy Valley in Yosemite National Park. In the ensuing political struggle, NPCA pushed for an amendment to the water power law that would prohibit such projects in all national parks. A compromise produced only a partial victory: the ban applied to the parks then in existence, but not to parks yet to be established. As a result, each new park's enabling legislation would have to expressly stipulate that the park was exempt from the commission's authority to develop hydropower projects. Yet this success, even if partial, was significant.

Also in the 1920s, NPCA successfully urged establishment of new national parks: Shenandoah, Great Smoky Mountains, Carlsbad Caverns, Bryce Canyon, and a park that later became Kings Canyon, as well as an expanded Sequoia. The association also pushed to expand Yellowstone, Grand Canyon, and Rocky Mountain national parks, pointing out that "the boundaries of the older parks were often established arbitrarily, following ruler lines drawn in far-away offices." The association continues to advocate such topographically and ecologically oriented boundary improvements for many parks.

In 1930, the establishment of Colonial National Historical Park and the George Washington Birthplace National Monument signaled a broadening of the National Park System to places of primarily historical rather than environmental importance. A number of other historical areas, such as Civil War battlefields, were soon transferred from U.S. military jurisdiction to the National Park Service, and NPCA accurately predicted that this new category of parks "will rapidly surpass, in the number of units, its world-celebrated scenic" parks. Today, there are roughly 200 historical parks out of the total of 378 units. NPCA also pushed to add other units, including Everglades National Park, which was finally established in 1947.

A new category of National Park System units was initiated with the establishment of Cape Hatteras National Seashore in North Carolina. However, in spite of NPCA opposition, Congress permitted public hunting in the seashore—a precedent that subsequently opened the way to allow this consumptive resource use in other national seashores, national lakeshores, national rivers, and national preserves. With the exception of traditional, subsistence hunting in Alaska national preserves, NPCA continues to oppose hunting in all national parks and monuments.

In contrast to its loss at Cape Hatteras, NPCA achieved a victory regarding Kings Canyon National Park as a result of patience and tenacity. When the park was established in 1940, two valleys—Tehipite and Cedar Grove—were left out of the park as a concession to hydroelectric power and irrigation interests. A few years later, however, as the result of concerted efforts by the association and other environmental groups, these magnificently scenic valleys were added to the park.

In 1942, the association took a major step in its public education mission when it began publishing *National Parks*. This award-winning, full-color magazine contains news, editorials, and feature articles that help to inform members about the parks, threats facing them, and opportunities for worthy new parks and offers readers a chance to participate in the protection and enhancement of the National Park System.

In one of the most heavily publicized park-protection battles of the 1950s, NPCA and other groups succeeded in blocking construction of two hydroelectric power dams that would have inundated the spectacularly scenic river canyons in Dinosaur National Monument. In the 1960s, an even bigger battle erupted over U.S. Bureau of Reclamation plans to build two dams in the Grand Canyon. But with the cooperative efforts of a number of leading environmental organizations and tremendous help from the news media, these schemes were defeated, and Grand Canyon National Park was expanded.

In 1980, the National Park System nearly tripled in size with the passage of the Alaska National Interest Lands Conservation Act (ANILCA). One of the great milestones in the history of American land conservation, ANILCA established ten new, and expanded three existing, national park units in Alaska. This carefully crafted compromise also recognized the special circumstances of Alaska and authorized subsistence hunting, fishing, and gathering by rural residents as well as special access provisions on most units. The challenge of ANILCA is to achieve a balance of interests that are often in conflict. Currently, NPCA is working to protect sensitive park areas and wildlife from inappropriate development of roads and unregulated motorized use, and to ensure that our magnificent national parks in Alaska always offer the sense of wildness, discovery, and adventure that Congress intended.

In 1981, the association sponsored a conference to address serious issues affecting the welfare of the National Park System. The following year, NPCA published a book on this theme called *National Parks in Crisis.* In the 1980s and 1990s, as well, the association sponsored its nationwide "March for Parks" program in conjunction with Earth Day in April. Money raised from the hundreds of marches funds local park projects, including improvement and protection priorities and educational projects in national, state, and local parks.

NPCA's landmark nine-volume document, *National Park System Plan,* was issued in 1988. It contained proposals for new parks and park expansions, assessments of threats to park resources and of research needs, explorations of the importance of interpretation to the visitor's quality of experience, and issues relating to the internal organization of the National Park Service. Two years later, the two-volume *Visitor Impact Management* was released. This document found favor within the National Park Service because of its pragmatic discussions of "carrying capacity" and visitor-impact management methodology and its case studies. In 1993, *Park Waters in Peril* was released, focusing on threats seriously jeopardizing water resources and presenting a dozen case studies.

The association has become increasingly concerned about the effect of noise on the natural quiet in the parks. NPCA has helped formulate restrictions on flightseeing tours over key parts of the Grand Canyon; urged special restrictions on tour flights over Alaska's national parks; supported a ban on tour flights over other national parks such as Yosemite; expressed opposition to plans for construction of major new commercial airports close to Mojave National Preserve and Petroglyph National Monument; opposed the recreational use of snowmobiles in some parks and advocated restrictions on their use in others; and supported regulations prohibiting the use of personal watercraft on lakes in national parks.

Other association activities of the late 20th century have included helping to block development of a major gold mining operation that could have seriously impaired Yellowstone National Park; opposing a coal mine near Zion National Park that would have polluted Zion Canyon's North Fork of the Virgin River; objecting to proposed lead mining that could pollute the Ozark National Scenic Riverways; opposing a major waste dump adjacent to Joshua Tree National Park; and helping to defeat a proposed U.S. Department of Energy nuclear waste dump adjacent to Canyonlands National Park and on lands worthy of addition to the park. NPCA is currently proposing the completion of this national park with the addition of 500,000 acres. This proposal to double the size of the park would extend protection across the entire Canyonlands Basin. NPCA has also continued to work with the Everglades Coalition and others to help formulate meaningful ways of restoring the seriously impaired Everglades ecosystem; is urging protection of New Mexico's geologically and scenically outstanding Valles Caldera, adjacent to Bandelier National Monument; and is pushing for the installation of scrubbers on air-polluting coal-fired power plants in the Midwest and upwind from the Grand Canyon.

The association, in addition, is continuing to seek meaningful solutions to traffic congestion and urbanization on the South Rim of the Grand Canyon and in Yosemite Valley; is opposing construction of a six-lane highway through Petroglyph National Monument that would destroy sacred Native American cultural assets; and is fighting a plan to build a new road through Denali National Park. NPCA has supported re-establishment of such native wildlife as the gray wolf at Yellowstone and desert bighorn sheep at Capitol Reef and other desert parks, as well as urging increased scientific research that will enable the National Park Service to more effectively protect natural ecological processes in the future. The association is also continuing to explore a proposal to combine Organ Pipe Cactus National Monument and Cabreza Prieta National Wildlife Refuge into a Sonoran Desert National Park, possibly in conjunction with Mexico's Pinacate Biosphere Reserve.

In 1994, on the occasion of NPCA's 75th anniversary, the association sponsored a major conference on the theme "Citizens Protecting America's Parks: Joining Forces for the Future." As a result, NPCA became more active in recruiting a more racially and socially diverse group of park protectors. Rallying new constituencies for the parks helped NPCA in 1995 to defeat a bill that would have called for Congress to review national parks for possible closure. NPCA was also instrumental in the passage of legislation to establish the National Underground Railroad Network to Freedom.

In January 1999, NPCA hosted another major conference, this time focusing on the need for the park system, and the Park Service itself, to be relevant, accessible, and open to all Americans. The conference led to the creation of a number of partnership teams between national parks and minority communities. In conjunction with all this program activity, the association experienced its greatest growth in membership, jumping from about 24,000 in 1980 to nearly 400,000 in the late 1990s.

As NPCA and its committed Board of Trustees, staff, and volunteers face the challenges of park protection in the 21st century, the words of the association's past president, Wallace W. Atwood, in 1929 are as timely now as then:

> All who join our association have the satisfaction that comes only from unselfish acts; they will help carry forward a consistent and progressive program . . . for the preservation and most appropriate utilization of the unique wonderlands of our country. Join and make this work more effective.

Each of us can help nurture one of the noblest endeavors in the entire history of mankind—the national parks idea that began so many years ago at Yellowstone and has spread and blossomed around the world. Everyone can help make a difference in determining just how well we succeed in protecting the priceless and irreplaceable natural and cultural heritage of the National Park System and passing it along unimpaired for the generations to come.

Big Cypress National Preserve

▲ Quill leaf air plant

Big Cypress National Preserve

HCR 61, Box 110
Ochopee, FL 33943
941-695-4111

This 716,000-acre national preserve adjoining Everglades National Park in south Florida protects a subtropical area containing sandy, slash-pine-covered islands, mixed hardwood hammocks (islands), bald cypress domes and swamp, wet and dry prairies, saw grass marsh, sloughs, and estuarine mangrove forests. The preserve is named for an abundant, small-leafed variant of the bald cypress known as the pond cypress, a deciduous conifer tree with a broadly buttressed trunk and woody root "knees" that protrude above the water. This tree (*Taxodium distichum* var. *nutans*) favors shallow swampy habitat in the southeastern United States.

The preserve's primeval environment was once the ancestral homeland of Seminole and Miccosukee Indians. It is now a sanctuary for an abundance of wildlife, including the alligator, black bear, whitetail deer, the endangered Florida panther, river otter, mink, raccoon, opossum, armadillo, anhinga, herons, great and snowy egrets, white ibis, wood stork, mottled duck, limpkin, wild turkey, bobwhite, swallow-tailed kite, osprey, barred owl, pileated and red-bellied woodpeckers, the rare red-cockaded woodpecker, Carolina wren, brown thrasher, mockingbird, catbird, numerous warblers, and cardinal. Big Cypress Swamp's nutrient-rich mixture of fresh- and saltwater habitats also supports an abundance of marine life, including

▼*Bald cypress and common egret, Big Cypress National Preserve, Florida*

shrimp, snapper, snook, and other fish. In fact, one of the main purposes for establishing the preserve in 1974 was to create a sizable protected freshwater area that would help safeguard the threatened mangrove and estuarine ecosystems, down-watershed in the Everglades.

PRACTICAL INFORMATION

When to Go

The park is open year-round. Summers are hot and humid, with frequent daytime thundershowers. Temperatures rarely fall below the mid-50s throughout the year, and skies are a combination of clouds and sun for the majority of days. The dry season runs from around mid-December to mid-April.

How to Get There

By Car: The Tamiami Trail (U.S. Route 41) runs through the southern part of the preserve (west of Miami and southeast of Naples); and Alligator Alley (I-75 and a toll road) runs through the northern part of the preserve (west of Fort Lauderdale and east of Naples).

By Air: Miami International Airport (305-876-7000) and Southwest Florida International Airport in Fort Myers (813-768-1000) are served by most major airlines.

By Train: Amtrak (800-872-7245) has stops in Miami.

By Bus: Greyhound Lines (800-231-2222) has stops in Miami and Naples.

Fees and Permits

There are no entrance fees. Permits for the use of off-road-vehicles are required and can be obtained at the visitor center. Permits for hunting and fishing are also required and can be purchased by contacting the Florida Game and Fresh Water Fish Commission at 904-488-1960.

Visitor Center

Big Cypress Visitor Center: open daily except Christmas. Interpretive wildlife exhibits, a short audiovisual program, and publications.

Facilities

Picnic areas and campgrounds are available.

Handicapped Accessibility

Picnic areas and restrooms are wheelchair-accessible.

Medical Services

First aid is available at the visitor center. Hospitals are located in Naples and Miami, 20 to 30 miles away.

Pets

Pets must be leashed or otherwise physically restrained at all times.

Safety and Regulations

For your safety and enjoyment and for the protection of the park, please follow these regulations and suggestions:

- Special Florida Game Management Area regulations apply to fishing and public hunting; contact the visitor center for information.

- Off-road vehicles are restricted to certain areas and trails.

- Visitors are cautioned to be alert for poisonous snakes, poison ivy, and poison wood, especially on the hammocks (islands). Mosquitoes are prevalent during the summer.

- Use extreme caution when driving off the improved roadways because hot catalytic converters can ignite fires.

- Federal law prohibits collecting archaeological artifacts or disturbing historic sites or Indian mounds.

ACTIVITIES

Options include hiking, birdwatching, interpreter-guided "swamp tromps," bicycling, canoeing (two canoe trails lead into Everglades National Park), camping, fishing, public hunting in part of the preserve during the designated season, and off-road-vehicle use by swamp buggy, airboat, and ATV. Further information is provided in the National Park Service's newspaper, *Visitor's Guide to National Parks and Preserves of South Florida.*

Hiking Trails

Some of the available trails include: **Turner River Trail**, a short, self-guided interpretive trail beginning just east of Ochopee on U.S. Route 41; **Tree Snail Hammock Nature Trail**, a short, self-guided trail beginning opposite the Environmental Education Center on the 26-mile, unpaved Loop Road (State Route 94); and **Florida Trail**, a 31-mile stretch of this national scenic trail that winds through the preserve.

OVERNIGHT STAYS

Lodging and Dining

There are no lodging or dining facilities within the preserve. Accommodations and services are available in such communities as Everglades City, Naples, and Miami.

Campgrounds

A number of primitive, front-country campgrounds without water or facilities are available. All of them allow tent camping, and most accommodate motor homes. Dona Drive campground has water; a fee is charged to stay there. Campgrounds are usually at capacity during the winter months. The visitor center offers further information.

Backcountry Camping

Backcountry camping is permitted throughout the preserve. However, most locations are too wet to camp there. Two primitive campsites, without potable water, are located along the Florida Trail, a national scenic trail.

FLORA AND FAUNA (Partial Listings)

(See Everglades National Park.)

NEARBY POINTS OF INTEREST

The area around Big Cypress National Preserve offers other fascinating natural and cultural attractions that can be enjoyed as day trips or overnight excursions. Everglades National Park adjoins the southern boundary of the preserve; the Florida Panther National Wildlife Refuge and the Fakahatchee Strand State Preserve are to the west; and the National Audubon Society's Corkscrew Swamp Sanctuary is to the northwest. Biscayne National Park and John Pennekamp Coral Reef State Park are located along the southeast coast of Florida.

▲ *Brilliant fall foliage*

BLUE RIDGE PARKWAY

400 BB&T Building
Asheville, NC 28801-3412
704-271-4779

The Blue Ridge Parkway, encompassing 87,992 acres and extending 469 miles along the crest of the southern Appalachian Mountains, links Shenandoah National Park's Skyline Drive in Virginia with Great Smoky Mountains National Park in Tennessee and North Carolina. This scenic route provides spectacular panoramas of richly forested, long parallel mountain ranges, jumbles of mountains, and deep valleys. Among the highlights along this beautiful parkway are an abundance of wildlife, streams and waterfalls, displays of spring and summer wildflowers, brilliant colors of autumn foliage, and the heritage of the early pioneering mountain people. In 1933, initial parkway construction funds were allocated, under authority of the National Industrial Recovery Act, as one of many public works projects throughout the country that helped stimulate economic recovery from the Great Depression. The roadway's winding route was sensitively designed by landscape architects; construction commenced in 1935; and in 1936 the parkway was established as a unit of the National Park System. In addition to the road itself, 18 recreation areas range in size from 250 to 6,000 acres.

OUTSTANDING FEATURES

Among the many outstanding features of the park along the **Virginia segment** are the following: **Humpback Rocks**, a reconstructed pioneer mountain farm, including a cabin, outbuildings, .75-mile hiking trail to the rocks, and visitor center; **Ravens Roost**, an area affording vistas of Torry Mountain and the Shenandoah Valley to the west; **Sherando Lake**, a recreation area near the parkway in adjacent George Washington National Forest; **Whetstone Ridge**, a ridge of sandstone from which early settlers made high-quality, fine-grained whetstone for sharpening knives; **Yankee Horse Ridge**, the spot where a Union soldier's horse allegedly fell during the Civil War and had to be shot; nearby are a walk to Wigwam Falls and a reconstructed spur line of an old logging railroad; **Kanawha Canal**, a restored canal lock that is a historical remnant of the nearly 200-mile transportation canal constructed westward from Richmond along the James River through the Blue Ridge to Buchanan; completed in 1851, the canal was originally planned to extend to the Ohio River but, as with other early 19th-century canal-building projects, this one was halted when the canal era ended with the expansion of railroads; **Onion Mountain Overlook**, a short loop walk leading through an area of rhododendrons and mountain laurel; **Fallingwater Cascades**, a waterfall reached by a short loop walk; **Peaks of Otter**, a range including Sharp Top and Flat Top, which cradle between them a small mountain valley that once held a community of about 20 families, including a now-restored historical farm; shuttle service for a fee is available to Sharp Top, from which specatcular views are possible; **Roanoke River Gorge**, a deep gorge visible from the nearby **Roanoke Valley Overlook**, which also provides a panoramic view of the largest community along the parkway; **Smart View**, an overlook named for the "right smart view" said to be available from an 1890s trail cabin; **Rocky Knob**, a formation resembling the cresting of a wave that looks into Rock Castle Gorge with its remnants of former farmsteads; and **Mabry Mill**, a picturesque, waterwheel-driven gristmill used from 1910 to 1935 to grind corn and run a sawmill; a blacksmith shop is located nearby and living-history demonstrations of all these activities are presented.

Among the many outstanding features of the park along the **North Carolina segment** are the following: **Cumberland Knob**, a delightful area for strolling through fields and woods; **Brinegar Cabin**, a weaver's cabin dating from around 1880 and occupied until the 1930s where weaving demonstrations are now presented and handmade crafts are for sale; **Doughton Park**, an expanse of high mountain meadows and a good place to spot

BLUE RIDGE PARKWAY

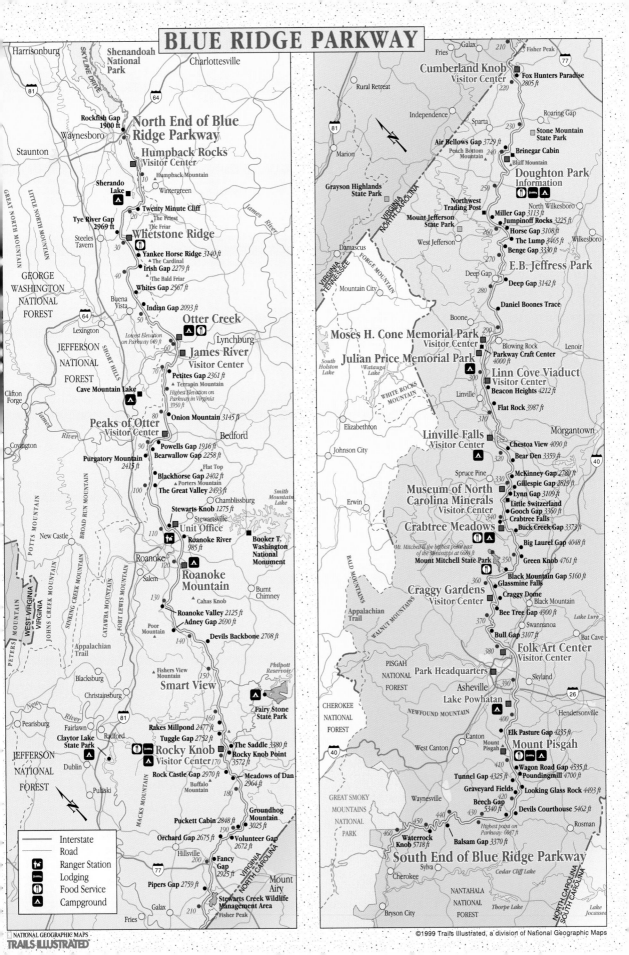

Harrisonburg
Shenandoah National Park
Charlottesville
SKYLINE DRIVE
Galax
Fries
Fisher Peak
77

Rockfish Gap 1900 ft
North End of Blue Ridge Parkway
Waynesboro
Staunton
64
81

Cumberland Knob Visitor Center
Fox Hunters Paradise 2805 ft
220
Rural Retreat
Roaring Gap
210

Humpback Rocks Visitor Center
Sherando Lake
Humpback Mountain
Wintergreen
Twenty Minute Cliff
Tye River Gap 2969 ft
Steeles Tavern
Whetstone Ridge
Yankee Horse Ridge 3140 ft
The Priest
The Friar
The Cardinal
Irish Gap 2279 ft
The Bald Friar
Whites Gap 2567 ft
Buena Vista
Indian Gap 2093 ft
Otter Creek
Lowest Elevation on Parkway 649 ft
Lexington
James River Visitor Center
Lynchburg
Petites Gap 2361 ft
Terrapin Mountain
Highest Elevation on Parkway in Virginia 3950 ft
Cave Mountain Lake
Onion Mountain 3145 ft
Peaks of Otter Visitor Center
Bedford
Powells Gap 1916 ft
Bearwallow Gap 2258 ft
Purgatory Mountain 2415 ft
Flat Top
Blackhorse Gap 2402 ft
Porters Mountain
The Great Valley 2493 ft
Chamblissburg
Stewarts Knob 1275 ft
Stewartsville
Unit Office
Roanoke River 985 ft
Booker T. Washington National Monument
Roanoke
Salem
Roanoke Mountain
Burnt Chimney
Cahas Knob
Roanoke Valley 2125 ft
Adney Gap 2690 ft
Poor Mountain
Devils Backbone 2708 ft
Fishers View Mountain
Philpott Reservoir
Smart View
Fairy Stone State Park
Rakes Millpond 2477 ft
Tuggle Gap 2752 ft
Rocky Knob Visitor Center
The Saddle 3380 ft
Rocky Knob Point 3572 ft
Rock Castle Gap 2970 ft
Meadows of Dan 2964 ft
Buffalo Mountain
Groundhog Mountain 3025 ft
Puckett Cabin 2848 ft
Orchard Gap 2675 ft
Volunteer Gap 2672 ft
Hillsville
Fancy Gap 2925 ft
Pipers Gap 2759 ft
Mount Airy
Stewarts Creek Wildlife Management Area
Galax
Fries
Fisher Peak

GEORGE WASHINGTON NATIONAL FOREST
GREAT NORTH MOUNTAIN
LITTLE NORTH MOUNTAIN
SHORT HILLS
JEFFERSON NATIONAL FOREST
Clifton Forge
Covington
New Castle
WEST VIRGINIA
VIRGINIA
PETERS MOUNTAIN
POTTS MOUNTAIN
JOHNS CREEK MOUNTAIN
SINKING CREEK MOUNTAIN
CATAWBA MOUNTAIN
FORT LEWIS MOUNTAIN
BROAD RUN MOUNTAIN
Blacksburg
Christiansburg
New River
Pearisburg
Fairlawn
Radford
Claytor Lake State Park
Dublin
Pulaski
JEFFERSON NATIONAL FOREST
MACKS MOUNTAIN
81
77

Independence
Sparta
230
Stone Mountain State Park
Marion
Air Bellows Gap 3729 ft
Peach Bottom Mountain
Brinegar Cabin
Bluff Mountain
240
Doughton Park Information
250
Grayson Highlands State Park
Damascus
Mount Jefferson State Park
West Jefferson
Northwest Trading Post
North Wilkesboro
Miller Gap 3113 ft
Jumpinoff Rocks 3225 ft
Horse Gap 3108 ft
Wilkesboro
The Lump 3465 ft
Benge Gap 3330 ft
E.B. Jeffress Park
VIRGINIA TENNESSEE
VIRGINIA NORTH CAROLINA
FORGE MOUNTAIN
Mountain City
Deep Gap
Deep Gap 3142 ft
Daniel Boones Trace
Boone
260
270
280
Moses H. Cone Memorial Park Visitor Center
Blowing Rock
Lenoir
290
Julian Price Memorial Park
Parkway Craft Center 4000 ft
Linn Cove Viaduct Visitor Center
Beacon Heights 4212 ft
Linville
Flat Rock 3987 ft
South Holston Lake
Watauga Lake
WHITE ROCKS MOUNTAIN
Elizabethton
Johnson City
Linville Falls Visitor Center
Chestoa View 4090 ft
Bear Den 3359 ft
300
310
320
Morgantown
40
Spruce Pine
McKinney Gap 2780 ft
Gillespie Gap 2819 ft
Museum of North Carolina Minerals Visitor Center
Lynn Gap 3109 ft
Little Switzerland
Gooch Gap 3360 ft
Crabtree Falls
Buck Creek Gap 3373 ft
Crabtree Meadows
Big Laurel Gap 4048 ft
330
340
Erwin
Mt. Mitchell is the highest point east of the Mississippi at 6684 ft
Mount Mitchell State Park
Green Knob 4761 ft
350
360
Black Mountain Gap 5160 ft
Glassmine Falls
Craggy Gardens Visitor Center
Craggy Dome
Black Mountain
Bee Tree Gap 4900 ft
Swannanoa
Lake Lure
Bull Gap 3107 ft
Bat Cave
370
380
Folk Art Center Visitor Center
BALD MOUNTAINS
Appalachian Trail
WALNUT MOUNTAINS
PISGAH NATIONAL FOREST
Park Headquarters
Asheville
Skyland
390
Lake Powhatan
Hendersonville
26
NEWFOUND MOUNTAIN
Elk Pasture Gap 4235 ft
400
CHEROKEE NATIONAL FOREST
Canton
Mount Pisgah
West Canton
Mount Pisgah
Wagon Road Gap 4535 ft
Poundingmill 4700 ft
410
Tunnel Gap 4325 ft
Looking Glass Rock 4493 ft
Graveyard Fields
Beech Gap 5340 ft
420
Devils Courthouse 5462 ft
430
Waynesville
Highest point on Parkway 6047 ft
440
450
GREAT SMOKY MOUNTAINS NATIONAL PARK
460
Waterrock Knob 5718 ft
Balsam Gap 3370 ft
40
South End of Blue Ridge Parkway
Sylva
Rosman
Cherokee
Cedar Cliff Lake
NANTAHALA NATIONAL FOREST
Bryson City
Thorpe Lake
Lake Jocassee
NORTH CAROLINA SOUTH CAROLINA

Legend

— Interstate
— Road
Ranger Station
Lodging
Food Service
Campground

NATIONAL GEOGRAPHIC MAPS
TRAILS ILLUSTRATED

©1999 Trails Illustrated, a division of National Geographic Maps

whitetail deer; **Northwest Trading Post**, a post sponsored by the Northwest Development Association to support and sell traditional crafts made in North Carolina's 11 northwest counties; **Jumpinoff Rocks**, a beautiful viewpoint reached by a short woodland trail; **The Lump**, a view offering a panorama of forested foothills; **E. B. Jeffress Park**, an area from which one self-guided trail leads to the Cascades and another to a historical church and cabin; **Boone's Trace**, the trail that Daniel Boone blazed through the wilderness to Kentucky; **Moses H. Cone Memorial Park**, a beautiful, 3,600-acre estate with 20-room Flat Top Manor (now with a craft shop) and 25 miles of carriage roads, named for a late-19th-century textile magnate; **Julian Price Memorial Park**, a former retreat of a business executive, offering short trails and a lake; **Linn Cove Viaduct**, a waterway that skirts the side of 5,890-foot-high Grandfather Mountain; **Flat Rock**, a spot offering an outstanding view of Grandfather Mountain and Linville Valley; **Linville Falls**, waterfalls in the ruggedly scenic Linville River gorge reached by a trail through a stand of old-growth hemlocks and white pines; **Museum of North Carolina Minerals**, which provides interpretive exhibits on the state's mineral wealth; **Crabtree Meadows**, a grassy area from which a trail leads down to spectacular Crabtree Falls; **Mount Mitchell State Park**, at 6,684 feet above sea level, the highest point east of the Mississippi River; **Craggy Gardens**, a high mountain heath "bald" (one of many scattered through the southern Appalachians), which presents a magnificent scene of flowering purplish-pink Catawba rhododendrons in mid- to late June; **The Folk Art Center** near Asheville, which supports traditional and contemporary Appalachian regional crafts through its exhibits and sales; **Mount Pisgah**, a part of the Biltmore Estate, which became the first forestry school in the United States, in the Pisgah National Forest; **Devil's Courthouse**, a rocky mountaintop affording a grand view of the surrounding of Pisgah National Forest; **Richland Balsam**, at 6,047 feet, the highest point on the parkway, reached via a self-guided nature trail leading through a remnant spruce-fir forest; and **Waterrock Knob**, a spot that offers a panoramic view of Great Smoky Mountains National Park.

Note that many of these sites have their own visitor centers.

PRACTICAL INFORMATION

When to Go

The parkway motor road is open year-round, with sections sometimes closed in winter because of snow or ice. From May to October, all campgrounds, visitor centers, and concession facilities are open.

How to Get There

By Car: *From the north*—enter from Shenandoah National Park's Skyline Drive or from I-64 or U.S. Route 250 between Charlottesville and Waynesboro, Virginia. *From the south*—enter from Great Smoky Mountains National Park at U.S. Route 441. Among the highways that cross the parkway are U.S. Route 60 between Amherst and Lexington, Virginia; U.S. Route 501 between Lynchburg and Glasgow, Virginia; U.S. Routes 221/460 between Bedford and Roanoke, Virginia; U.S. Route 220 between Rocky Mount and Roanoke, Virginia; U.S. Route 58 between Stuart and Hillsville, Virginia; U.S. Route 52 between Mount Airy, North Carolina, and Hillsville, Virginia; U.S. Route 21 between Elkin and Sparta, North Carolina; U.S. Route 421 between Wilkesboro and Boone, North Carolina; U.S. Route 321 between Lenoir and Boone, North Carolina; U.S. Route 221 between Marion and Linville, North Carolina; U.S. Route 25 between Hendersonville and Asheville, North Carolina; and U.S. Routes 23/74 between Sylva and Waynesville, North Carolina.

Fees and Permits

There is no entrance fee to the parkway. Commercial vehicles are prohibited. Backcountry camping permits are available at visitor centers.

Visitor Centers, Museum, and Folk Art Center

Museum of North Carolina Minerals: open daily, except Thanksgiving, Christmas, and New Year's Day. Interpretive exhibits on North Carolina's mineral wealth.

Folk Art Center: open daily, except Thanksgiving, Christmas, and New Year's Day. Exhibits and sales of traditional and contemporary crafts of the Appalachian Region, interpretive programs, art gallery, library, and demonstrations.

Additional visitor centers are located in Virginia at Humpback Rocks, James River, Peaks of Otter, and Rocky Knob; and in North Carolina at Cumberland Knob, Moses H. Cone Memorial Park, Linn Cove Viaduct, Linville Falls, Craggy Gardens, and Waterrock Knob. Most are open May 1 through October, providing interpretive exhibits, programs, and publications.

Facilities

Available are lodging, restaurants, picnic areas, campgrounds, and service stations.

Handicapped Accessibility

Facilities along the parkway are in the development stage of meeting the Americans with Disabilities Act (ADA) standards. However, most have at least one means of access. Several sites in every campground, except Rocky Knob, along with most restrooms, visitor centers, and sites and restrooms at all picnic areas, are wheelchair-accessible. Contact individual facilities through the park's main number for details.

Medical Services

First aid is available from rangers. Hospitals are located in many communities along the parkway.

Pets

Pets must be leashed or otherwise physically restrained at all times.

Safety and Regulations

For your safety and enjoyment and for the protection of the park, please follow these regulations and suggestions:

- Visitors are urged to drive carefully, wear safety belts, and not exceed 45 miles per hour.

- Fires, including charcoal, are permitted only in campgrounds and picnic areas.

- The National Park Service asks that visitors not litter; use trash containers at parking and picnic areas.

- Do not swim in lakes and ponds within parkway boundaries (swimming areas are located in nearby recreation areas, state parks, and resorts). Only boats without motors or sails are permitted on Price Lake.

- Remember that feeding, disturbing, capturing, or hunting wildlife is illegal.

ACTIVITIES

Options include hiking, interpretive walks and talks, birdwatching, wildflower and autumn foliage viewing, picnicking, camping, fishing, and craft demonstrations. Canoes and boats are available for rental.

OVERNIGHT STAYS

Lodging and Dining

Lodging is provided from spring to autumn except at Peaks of Otter Lodge, which is open year-round. Reservations are recommended and can be made at the following locations:

Peaks of Otter Lodge, P.O. Box 489, Bedford, VA 24523; 540-586-1083.

Rocky Knob Cabins, c/o National Park Concessions, Rt. 1, Box 5, Meadows of Dan, VA 24120; 540-593-3503.

Bluffs Lodge, c/o National Park Concessions, Rt. 1, Box 266, Laurel Springs, NC 28644; 336-372-4499.

Pisgah Inn, P.O. Drawer 749, Waynesville, NC 28786; 828-235-8228.

Meals are served at Whetstone Ridge, Otter Creek, Peaks of Otter, Mabry Mill, Doughton Park, Crabtree Meadows, and Mount Pisgah. Accommodations and dining facilities are also available in nearby communities.

Campgrounds

Campgrounds are open from about May 1 through October or into early November, depending on weather conditions. Facilities are limited in winter. Water is available at all campgrounds, but flush toilets are provided only from May through October; pit toilets are available otherwise. All campgrounds operate on a first-come, first-served basis.

Backcountry Camping

Backcountry camping is available year-round at designated campsites in Rock Castle Gorge and Basin Cove only, operating on a first-come, first-served basis. Free permits are required.

FLORA AND FAUNA (Partial Listings)

Mammals: black bear, whitetail deer, woodchuck, raccoon, opossum, spotted and striped skunks, eastern cottontail, eastern chipmunk, and gray, red, and flying squirrels.

Birds: woodcock, ruffed grouse, bobwhite, red-tailed and broad-winged hawks, turkey vulture, barred and great horned owls, mourning dove, yellow-billed cuckoo, whippoorwill, ruby-throated hummingbird, woodpeckers (pileated, downy, hairy, and red-bellied), flicker, great-crested and Acadian flycatchers, eastern wood pewee, eastern phoebe, chimney swift, barn swallow, crow, raven, blue jay, black-capped and Carolina chickadees, tufted titmouse, white-breasted and red-breasted nuthatches, brown creeper, golden-crowned kinglet, winter and Carolina wrens, brown thrasher, catbird, mockingbird, robin, veery, Swainson's and wood thrushes, eastern bluebird, cedar waxwing, red-eyed vireo, warblers (yellow-rumped, Canada, black-throated green, black-and-white, black-throated blue, chestnut-sided, blackburnian, yellow, hooded, northern parula, and pine), American redstart, ovenbird, yellow-breasted chat, scarlet tanager, sparrows (white-throated, chipping, field, and song), rufous-sided towhee, dark-eyed junco, rose-breasted grosbeak, indigo bunting, cardinal, purple finch, and American goldfinch.

Trees, Shrubs, and Flowers: pines (eastern white, Virginia, and pitch), red spruce, eastern and Carolina hemlocks, Fraser fir, cucumber tree, umbrella magnolia, tulip tree (yellow poplar), sassafras, witch hazel, hackberry, hickories (mockernut, shagbark, and pignut), beech, oaks (white, chestnut, northern red, black, and scarlet), sweet and yellow birches, American basswood, sourwood, black cherry, American mountain ash, eastern redbud, black locust, flowering dogwood, American holly, yellow buckeye, maples (mountain, striped, red, and sugar), white ash, the spectacular Catawba rhododendron (purple or rosy-purple flowers), Carolina or dwarf rhododendron (reddish-purple flowers), rosebay rhododendron (white or pinkish-white flowers), mountain laurel, flame azalea, shadbush, stiff gentian, lilies (bead, trout, and Turk's-cap), fire pink, a number of trilliums and violets, goldenrods, cardinal flower, Solomon's-seal, false Solomon's-seal, jack-in-the-pulpit, Mayapple, bluet, Dutchman's-breeches, columbine, spring beauty, bloodroot, black-eyed Susan, coneflower, and asters.

NEARBY POINTS OF INTEREST

The area surrounding the parkway offers many other fascinating natural and historical attractions that can be enjoyed as day trips or overnight excursions. Shenandoah and Great Smoky Mountains national parks lie at opposite ends of the parkway. The Booker T. Washington National Monument is just east of Roanoke, Virginia, and the Carl Sandburg Home National Historic Site is just east of the parkway near Hendersonville, North Carolina. Fairy Stone and Claytor Lake state parks are located northeast and west of Rocky Knob, respectively. The Stewarts Creek Wildlife Management Area is just north of Cumberland Knob. Stone Mountain State Park is northeast, and Mount Jefferson and Grayson Highlands state parks are southwest of Doughton Park. George Washington, Jefferson, Pisgah, and Nantahala national forests border stretches of the parkway.

Cape Hatteras National Seashore

▲ Ocracoke Lighthouse

Cape Hatteras National Seashore

**Route 1, Box 675
Manteo, NC 27954-2708
252-473-2111**

This 30,319-acre national seashore along the Atlantic coast of North Carolina protects a long stretch of narrow barrier islands on the Outer Banks, with their sandy beaches, sand dunes, salt marsh, and wind-sculpted woodlands of live oaks and other trees. The seashore includes much of Hatteras Island, the southern end of Bodie Island to the north, and most of the smaller, more isolated Ocracoke Island to the southwest. These islands contain a wild beauty, but also a grim history that has earned them the epithet "The Graveyard of the Atlantic," for more than 600 known shipwrecks lie scattered about offshore as evidence of the hazards of shoals and storms. These barrier islands are also in an uneasy alliance between land and sea, with the ocean constantly eroding, rebuilding, and changing their configuration. The national seashore was established in 1953. Nearly 6,000 acres within its boundaries are designated the Pea Island National Wildlife Refuge.

OUTSTANDING FEATURES

Among the many outstanding features of the park are the following: **Coquina Beach**, the area where the shipwreck *Laura A. Barnes* lies not far from where it ran aground in 1921; **Pea Island National Wildlife Refuge**, a 6,000-acre protected area that provides habitat for many species of waterfowl and other migrating birds; **Ocracoke Island**, an isolated island with a small harbor village, where the pirate Blackbeard often hid from his pursuers; **Cape Hatteras Lighthouse**, a black-and-white, spiral-striped monument built in 1870 and the tallest lighthouse in the United States; and the **historic U.S. lifesaving service stations** in Rodanthe and just north

of Avon, with re-enactments of early rescue drills performed weekly at the Chicamacomico Station in Rodanthe.

PRACTICAL INFORMATION

When to Go

The park is open year-round. Summer, always popular for beach visits, can be very hot and humid, as well as bug-filled later in the season. Winter is also humid, and northerly winds can make the weather feel much colder than temperatures indicate. Late spring is generally quite comfortable, with cool breezes and mild temperatures.

How to Get There

By Car: From the Norfolk, Virginia, area, drive southeast on Virginia and North Carolina Routes 168 to Barco; then southeast 67 miles on U.S. Route 158 through Kill Devil Hills and Nags Head on Bodie Island; and to the national seashore entrance at the junction of State Route 12. From Williamston, North Carolina, drive east 88 miles on U.S. Route 64 through Manns Harbor across the bridge to Roanoke Island, then across the bridge to Bodie Island and the seashore entrance at the junction of State Route 12.

By Air: Norfolk International Airport (804-857-3200) is served by most major carriers. Dare County Regional Airport (919-473-2600) is located at the north end of Roanoke Island, just west of Nags Head.

By Train: Amtrak (800-872-7245) has stops in Rocky Mount and Wilson, North Carolina, and Norfolk, Virginia.

By Bus: Greyhound Lines (800-231-2222) has stops in Rocky Mount, North Carolina.

By Boat: Toll ferries run from Cedar Island (919-225-3551) and Swanquarter (919-926-1111) to Ocracoke Island (reservations recommended). A free ferry runs daily year-round between Hatteras and Ocracoke islands.

Fees and Permits

There are no entrance fees.

CAPE HATTERAS NATIONAL SEASHORE

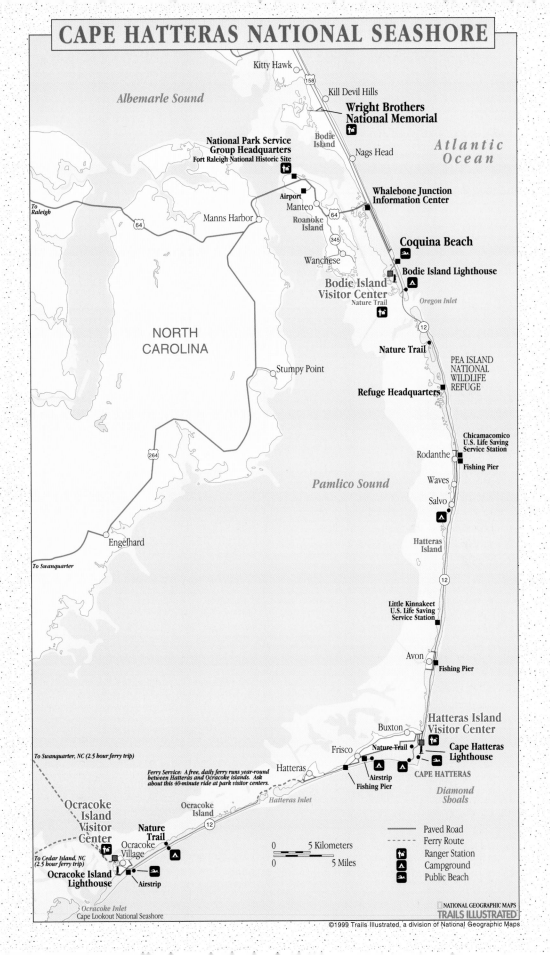

Kitty Hawk

158

Albemarle Sound

Kill Devil Hills

Wright Brothers National Memorial

Bodie Island

Nags Head

Atlantic Ocean

National Park Service Group Headquarters
Fort Raleigh National Historic Site

Airport

Manteo

Whalebone Junction Information Center

64

Roanoke Island

To Raleigh

64

Manns Harbor

345

Coquina Beach

Wanchese

Bodie Island Lighthouse

Bodie Island Visitor Center

Nature Trail

Oregon Inlet

NORTH CAROLINA

Nature Trail

12

PEA ISLAND NATIONAL WILDLIFE REFUGE

Stumpy Point

Refuge Headquarters

Chicamacomico U.S. Life Saving Service Station

Rodanthe

Fishing Pier

Pamlico Sound

Waves

Salvo

Hatteras Island

Engelhard

264

To Swanquarter

12

Little Kinnakeet U.S. Life Saving Service Station

Avon

Fishing Pier

Hatteras Island Visitor Center

Buxton

Cape Hatteras Lighthouse

Frisco

Nature Trail

To Swanquarter, NC (2.5 hour ferry trip)

Ferry Service: A free, daily ferry runs year-round between Hatteras and Ocracoke islands. Ask about this 40-minute ride at park visitor centers.

Hatteras

Airstrip

Fishing Pier

CAPE HATTERAS

Diamond Shoals

Hatteras Inlet

Ocracoke Island Visitor Center

Ocracoke Island

Nature Trail

12

Ocracoke Village

To Cedar Island, NC (2.5 hour ferry trip)

Ocracoke Island Lighthouse

Airstrip

0   5 Kilometers
0   5 Miles

——— Paved Road
- - - Ferry Route
Ranger Station
Campground
Public Beach

Ocracoke Inlet
Cape Lookout National Seashore

Visitor Centers and Information Center

Hatteras Island Visitor Center: open daily, except Christmas. Information and interpretive services.

Ocracoke Island Visitor Center: open from Memorial Day to Columbus Day. Information and interpretive services.

Bodie Island Visitor Center: open from Memorial Day to Columbus Day. Information and interpretive services.

Whalebone Junction Information Center: open from Easter to Columbus Day.

Facilities

Available are a marina, cold showers, drinking water, picnic tables, fire grills, dump stations, and bathhouses.

Handicapped Accessibility

Visitor center parking lots, restrooms, and several sites at all campgrounds are wheelchair-accessible.

Medical Services

First aid is available in the park. Limited medical services are available in Ocracoke, Hatteras, Manteo, and Nags Head. The nearest hospital is in Elizabeth City, 80 miles away.

Pets

Pets are permitted but must remain physically restrained at all times; leashes must not exceed six feet.

Safety and Regulations

For your safety and enjoyment and for the protection of the park, please follow these regulations and suggestions:

- The National Park Service advises ocean swimming only when lifeguards are on duty. Swimmers are cautioned to be aware of strong currents and breaking waves.

- Be prepared with plenty of sunscreen and insect repellent.

- Bicyclists should use extreme caution, as there are no established bike trails in the park.

- Visitors should be alert for the danger of hurricanes and winter storms, which should not be taken lightly in this exposed coastal terrain.

ACTIVITIES

Options include hiking, birdwatching, beachcombing, camping, swimming, canoeing, sailing, surfing, snorkeling, wreck-diving, bicy-

cling, and surf-fishing. Further information is available in the park's newspaper, *In the Park*.

▲ *Sea oats, Coquina Beach, Cape Hatteras National Seashore, North Carolina*

OVERNIGHT STAYS

Lodging and Dining

There are no lodging or dining facilities within the seashore. Nearby communities have ade-quate facilities. Contact the Dare County Tourist Bureau or the Outer Banks Chamber of Commerce (800-446-6262).

Campgrounds

There are four campgrounds: Oregon Inlet, Cape Point, Frisco, and Ocracoke.

Reservations for camping at Ocracoke in June, July, and August can be made through the National Park Reservation Service (800-365-CAMP). All other campsites are available on a first-come, first-served basis.

FLORA AND FAUNA (Partial Listings)

Mammals: whitetail deer, gray fox, mink, river otter, beaver, raccoon, striped skunk, opossum, marsh rabbit, eastern cottontail, gray and fox squirrels, eastern chipmunk, bottlenose dolphin, and humpback whale.

Birds: shearwater (sooty, Cory's, and Audubon's), black-capped petrel, petrels (band-rumped storm, Wilson's storm, and white-faced storm), white-tailed tropicbird, brown pelican, northern gannet, double-crested cormorant, tricolored and great blue herons, cattle and great egrets, tundra swan, snow and Canada geese, brant, gadwall, American wigeon, redhead, ring-necked duck, scoters (black, white-winged, and surf), bufflehead, red-breasted and hooded mergansers, American oystercatcher, avocet, black-necked stilt, plovers (piping, Wilson's, semipalmated, and black-bellied), willet, dunlin, sanderling, western and least sandpipers, gulls (laughing, ring-billed, herring, and great black-backed), terns (Forster's, gull-billed, least, royal, bridled, and sooty), black skimmer, northern harrier,

kestrel, belted kingfisher, tree and barn swallows, fish crow, Carolina wren, robin, catbird, warblers (orange-crowned, northern parula, and yellow-rumped), common yellowthroat, cardinal, rufous-sided towhee, sparrows (sharp-tailed, seaside, savannah, song, white-throated, and swamp), eastern meadowlark, red-winged blackbird, and boat-tailed grackle.

Trees, Shrubs, Flowers, and Grasses: loblolly pine, eastern redcedar, live oak, a variety of holly called yaupon, American hornbeam, wax myrtle, beach plum, serviceberry, bearberry, cattail, duckweed, eelgrass, seaside goldenrod, maritime gerardia, morning glory, sea oats, and American beach grass.

NEARBY POINTS OF INTEREST

The area surrounding the seashore offers other fascinating natural and cultural attractions that can be enjoyed as day trips or overnight excursions. Cape Lookout National Seashore is directly to the south. Fort Raleigh National Historic Site and Wright Brothers National Memorial are eight miles west and nine miles north, respectively, of Whalebone Junction. Jockey's Ridge State Park is just north of Nags Head; slightly farther, over the border and into Virginia, are Colonial National Historical Park and Jamestown National Historic Site.

EVERGLADES NATIONAL PARK

▲ Great blue heron

Everglades National Park

40001 State Road 9336
Homestead, FL 33034-6733
305-242-7700

This 1.5-million-acre national park at the southern tip of Florida encompasses an ecologically rich but seriously threatened subtropical wilderness, including the largest expanse of freshwater marshland in the world. This water enters the park from the north and flows slowly across a broad expanse from northeast to southwest, through the vast prairie marshland dominated by the Jamaica sawgrass, which is actually not a true grass but a grasslike sedge (*Cladium jamaicense*). Picturesque, jungly hardwood hammocks also dot this marshland. These slightly elevated, hump-shaped tree islands range in size from a few feet across to a few acres, and support such species as gumbo-limbo, mahogany, strangler fig, false mastic, willow bustic, poisonwood, palms, and the Spanish-moss-festooned live oak, along with orchids, bromeliads, and Boston fern.

The water leaving the Everglades gradually drains into rivers that flow to the Gulf of Mexico, creating a fringe of coastal mangrove swamp where the freshwater merges with saltwater. Other habitats include pinelands, where slash pine, the shrubby saw palmetto, and 30 species of endemic plants are found; clumps of trees called "heads," some dominated by cabbage palms, red bay, or cocoplum; a few stands of bald cypress; coastal marsh; coastal prairie; and estuarine and marine areas in Florida Bay and along the gulf coast with many little mangrove islands known as "keys" (from the Spanish *cayo*). The flora represents a unique merging of North American temperate and West Indies species, while the remarkably diverse flora and fauna are completely water-dependent, surviving and thriving in the natural seasonal rhythm of summer's deluges and winter's drought.

This rhythm has, however, been increasingly and severely disrupted for many decades as 1,400 miles of dikes, levees, and canals have intercepted and drawn off much of the vital flow of water to serve south Florida's rapidly expanding urban population and agri-cultural development. As more and more water has been diverted for human needs, the health of the fragile Everglades ecosystem has sharply declined since 1947, when the late Marjory Stoneman Douglas's *The Everglades: River of Grass* was published. That book was both her eloquent description of this unique area and a prescient warning that unrestrained urban and other commercial development could ultimately destroy this irreplaceable treasure. Since the national park was established that same year and the U.S. Army Corps of Engineers simultaneously began building a massive network of flood-control and water diversion projects upwatershed from the park, the populations of such wading birds as herons, egrets, storks, and ibises have plummeted to a mere 10 percent of their former abundance. Where even in the 1970s visitors could still be enthralled with the sight of large flocks of hundreds, if not thousands, of these magnificent birds, today there are perhaps only a few dozen at any time. Some other wildlife species, such as the Florida panther, American crocodile, manatee, and wood stork, are threatened with extinction.

This crisis has prompted one of the world's largest ecological restoration projects in history. As a founding member of the Everglades Coalition, NPCA has worked with other groups and agencies to urge actions to restore the collapsing Everglades ecosystem before it is too late. The two most urgent priorities are the restoration of a sufficient natural flow of water through the park and the cleanup of ecologically harmful phosphates, nitrates, and pesticides, draining from federally subsidized agricultural lands north of the park. Ironically, the same Corps of Engineers that built the dikes, levees, and canals is now directed by Congress to take the lead in the unprecedented multi-billion-dollar, 15-to-20-year South Florida Everglades Restoration Project. While those efforts proceed, NPCA has also helped fund a plan to diversify the gene pool of the Florida panther; urged an end to federal subsidies of Florida's politically powerful sugar industry, which is a major polluter of the Everglades waters; and helped raise national awareness of this environmental crisis. Everglades National Park has been given the honor of two international designations: a Biosphere Reserve in 1976 and a World Heritage Site in 1979.

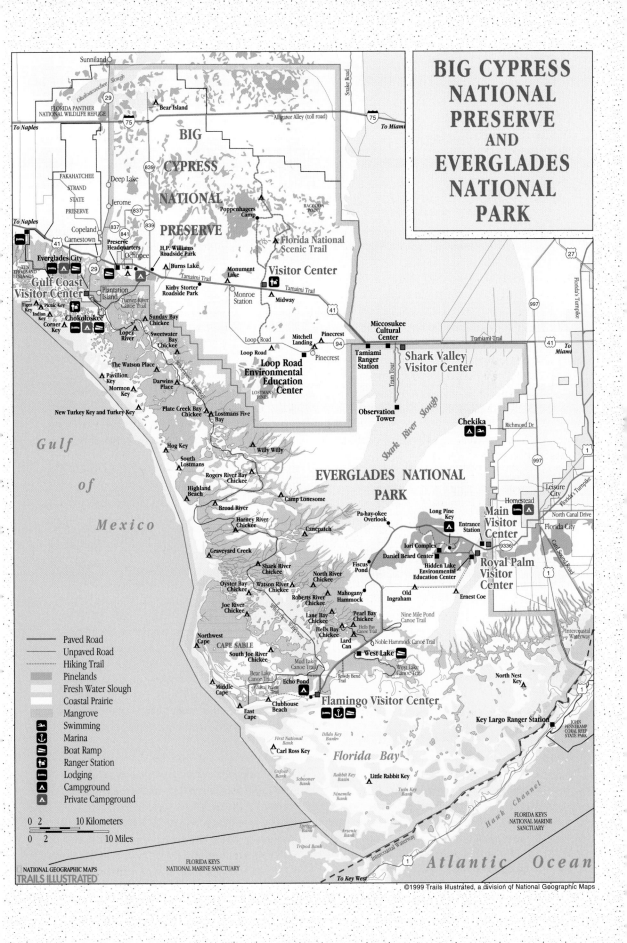

▲ *Anhinga, Everglades National Park, Florida*

OUTSTANDING FEATURES

Among the many outstanding features of the park are the following: **Royal Palm**, a spot where Gumbo Limbo and Anhinga trails provide outstanding opportunities to view plant and animal life in Taylor Slough, Royal Palm Hammock, and expanses of sawgrass prairie; **Long Pine Key**, a beautiful remnant of the once-extensive slash pine woodlands that covered the eastern edge of the Everglades prior to logging; **Pa-hay-okee Overlook**, an area with a boardwalk and observation tower that offers views of three distinct types of Everglades habitat—a hardwood hammock, a cypress strand, and sawgrass prairie marsh; **Mahogany Hammock**, a jungle-like hard-

wood island on which is the biggest living mahogany tree; **Flamingo**, an area with overnight accommodations, a marina, and other facilities and from which there are hiking trails, canoeing/kayaking routes, and interpreter-led boat cruises on Florida Bay and waterways winding through the mangrove swamp; **Shark Valley**, an expanse of sawgrass prairie south of the Shark River Visitor Center (at the northern edge of the park), reached by tram rides or bicycle, where a 65-foot observation tower overlooks an expanse of the Everglades and offers opportunities to view wading birds and alligators; **Ten Thousand Islands**, a pristine maze of islands and coastal mangroves in the north-western end of the park, reached by boat tours; and **Chokoloskee**, a 15-foot-high, 147-acre island of shells built by Indians and located in the park's northwestern end.

PRACTICAL INFORMATION

When to Go

The park is open year-round. Florida's dry season is normally from mid-December to mid-April. Winter temperatures are comfortable and range from the 40s at night to the 80s during the day. Summer is predictably hot and humid, with brief afternoon rainstorms, temperatures in the 80s and 90s, and an abundance of mosquitoes.

How to Get There

By Car: From U.S. Route 1, in Florida City, drive southwest ten miles on State Route 9336, to the park's main entrance and the Ernest F. Coe Visitor Center; from there, drive southwest 38 miles to the end of the road at Flamingo. The Shark Valley entrance is west 35 miles from downtown Miami, just south of the Tamiami Trail (U.S. Route 41). The Ten Thousand Islands entrance is 31 miles southeast of Naples or 80 miles west of downtown Miami on the Tamiami Trail (U.S. Route 41); proceed south on State Route 29 to reach the Gulf Coast Visitor Center and Chokoloskee.

By Air: Miami International Airport (305-876-7000) is about 35 miles from Homestead/Florida City, the gateway to the park.

By Train: Amtrak (800-872-7245) has stops in Miami.

By Bus: Greyhound Lines (800-231-2222) has stops in Homestead.

Fees and Permits

Entrance fees, valid for seven consecutive days, are $10 per vehicle and $5 per person at the main entrance. At the Shark Valley entrance, fees are $8 per vehicle and $4 per person. Freshwater and saltwater fishing requires a Florida fishing license, available at local bait and tackle shops. Backcountry camping

requires a free permit, available at the Everglades City and Flamingo ranger stations.

Visitor Centers

Ernest F. Coe Visitor Center: open daily. Interpretive exhibits, publications, maps, schedule of activities, and information on boat tours and canoe rentals.

Royal Palm Visitor Center: open daily. Interpretive displays on park ecosystems.

Flamingo Visitor Center: open daily. Interpretive natural history exhibits, publications, maps, information on sightseeing cruises and charter fishing, and boat, canoe, skiff, and bicycle rentals.

Shark Valley Visitor Center: open daily. Information, publications, tram tours, and bicycle rentals.

Gulf Coast Visitor Center: open daily. Interpretive exhibits of shore and marine ecology, publications, maps, canoe rentals, and information on interpretive boat cruises.

Facilities

Available are lodging, restaurant, marina, boat ramps, picnic areas, campgrounds, post office, swimming pool, grocery/camp store, cold showers, laundry, and service stations.

Handicapped Accessibility

Main and Shark Valley visitor centers, Flamingo Lodge and Visitor Center, some walking trails and boat tours, tram tours, and restrooms at campgrounds are all wheelchair-accessible. At least one site at each campground is reserved for the disabled and is located next to the accessible restrooms. In the backcountry, Pearl Bay Chickee is accessible. Contact the park for its detailed pamphlet on accessibility.

Medical Services

First aid is available at visitor centers. A hospital is located in Homestead.

Pets

Pets must be physically restrained and are not allowed on trails or in amphitheaters.

Safety and Regulations

For your safety and enjoyment and for the protection of the park, please follow these regulations and suggestions:

- Remember that feeding, disturbing, capturing, trapping, or hunting wildlife is illegal. The use of firearms is strictly forbidden. Visitors are cautioned to be alert for poisonous plants and snakes.

- Campers should use self-contained cooking stoves at backcountry campsites; ground fires are not permitted. Because of the fire hazard, smoking on trails is not allowed.

- The operation of personal watercraft (e.g., Jet Skis/Wave Runners) is prohibited on all park waters.

- Biting insects, such as mosquitoes, are always present and are unbearable during the summer rainy season. Campers should be equipped with insect repellent and netting.

- Swimming is strongly discouraged because of alligators, crocodiles, sharks, barracudas, and poor underwater visibility.

- Boaters should use extreme caution when in manatee areas because there is the risk of injuring or killing these slow-moving endangered creatures with boat propellers.

ACTIVITIES

Options include bird- and other wildlife-watching, boating, canoeing, kayaking, interpretive boat tours, hiking, interpretive walks and talks, "swamp tromps," tram tours, bicycling, picnicking, camping, and fishing, including charter fishing boats. Canoes, skiffs, boats, houseboats, and bicycles are available for rent. Further information is available in the park's newspaper, *Visitor's Guide to National Parks and Preserves of South Florida*.

Hiking Trails

Among the park's paths and hiking trails are the following:

At Royal Palm Visitor Center: **Anhinga Trail**, a .4-mile, paved, loop path and boardwalk leading into Taylor Slough and affording opportunities to see such wildlife as alligators, turtles, anhinga, herons, egrets, and gallinules; and **Gumbo-Limbo Trail**, a .4-mile, paved, loop path leading through lush Royal Palm Hammock with gumbo-limbo trees, royal palms, orchids, and ferns.

On Long Pine Key: **Pinelands Trail**, a .4-mile, paved, loop path through a beautiful area of slash pines with exposed, jagged limestone bedrock; and **Slash Pine Trail**, a seven-mile route winding between the Long Pine Key Campground and the main road.

Between Long Pine Key and Flamingo: **Pa-hay-okee Overlook Trail**, a quarter-mile boardwalk beginning at the end of the spur road and leading to an observation tower for a panorama of the glades; *Pa-hay-okee* is a Miccosukee word meaning "grassy waters"; **Mahogany Hammock Trail**, a .4-mile boardwalk, beginning at the end of the spur road and winding through a jungly hardwood hammock, where the largest living mahogany tree in the United States is growing; and **Mangrove Wilderness Trail**, a .4-mile boardwalk beginning at the park's main road and winding through a mangrove forest of red, white, black, and button mangroves.

In the Flamingo vicinity: **Eco Pond Loop Trail**, a half-mile loop, beginning and ending at the park's main road (near Flamingo), and leading around this freshwater pond where alligators, wading birds, and other wildlife can be viewed from a ramped viewing platform; sunrise and sunset visits can be especially rewarding; **Guy Bradley Trail**, a one-mile route along the shore of Florida Bay between Flamingo Visitor Center and the campground; **Bayshore Loop Trail**, a two-mile loop along the shore of Florida Bay, beginning and ending at the start of the Coast Prairie Trail at Flamingo Campground's Loop C; **Bear Lake Trail**, a 1.6-mile route beginning at the end of the Bear Lake spur road and leading to this lake through hardwood hammock and mangrove habitats; and **Coastal Prairie Trail**, a 7.5-mile route beginning at Flamingo Campground's Loop C and following an old road that passes by buttonwood mangroves and expanses of coastal prairie. A back-country permit is required for camping on this excursion.

At Shark Valley Visitor Center: **Bobcat Boardwalk and Otter Cave Trails**, short, self-guided interpretive trails beginning at the visitor center and offering the possibility, in winter and spring, of seeing the rare snail kite; and **Shark Valley Loop Road**, a 15-mile roadway beginning and ending at the visitor center; this route is used by the concession-operated tram service to Shark Valley Observation Tower and is also popular for bicycling and walking.

Canoe Trails

Among the park's canoe trails are the following:

In the Flamingo vicinity: **Nine Mile Pond Canoe Trail**, a 5.2-mile loop beginning and ending at the park's main road, winding through sawgrass marsh with scattered mangrove islands, and providing opportunities to see alligators and wading birds; **Noble Hammock Canoe Trail**, a two-mile loop beginning and ending at the park's main road and twisting through a maze of narrow, mangrove-bordered waterways and small ponds; **Hells Bay Canoe Trail**, a three-mile route beginning at the park's main road, winding and twisting through a series of narrow waterways and ponds to Lard Can, and continuing another half-mile to the camping site of Pearl Bay Chickee and two miles farther to Hells Bay Chickee; backcountry permits are required for camping along this route; **West Lake Canoe Trail**, a seven-mile route beginning at the park's main road, winding through a series of large lakes and narrow, mangrove-bordered waterways, and providing the possibility of seeing alligators and crocodiles; **Mud Lake Loop Canoe Trail**, a 6.8-mile loop beginning and ending at the park's main road and leading through Coot Bay, Mud Lake, the eastern end of Bear Lake Canal, a short portage, and the northern end of Buttonwood Canal back to Coot Bay; and **Bear Lake Canal Canoe Trail**, a 1.6-mile route beginning at the end of the Bear Lake spur road and paddling along this historic tree-lined canal (part of which is impassable during the dry season).

Near Gulf Coast Visitor Center: **Turner River Canoe Trail**, a 13-mile route beginning at the Tamiami Trail (U.S. Route 41) in Big Cypress National Preserve and ending at Chokoloskee Island at the northwest end of the park.

Between Gulf Coast Visitor Center and Flamingo: **Wilderness Waterway**, a well-marked, 99-mile, mangrove-wilderness route that winds through narrow waterways, rivers, and bays; a backcountry permit is required for this excursion that usually takes a week by canoe.

OVERNIGHT STAYS

Lodging and Dining

The Flamingo Lodge and Restaurant is the only lodging and dining facility within the park. It offers air-conditioned lodge rooms and cottages with kitchen facilities, a swimming pool, and other facilities. Visitors are advised to make reservations well in advance by contacting Flamingo Lodge and Marina, #1 Flamingo Lodge Highway, Flamingo, FL 33034; 800-600-3813 or 941-695-3101. Dinner reservations for the restaurant are also recommended. Lodging and dining facilities outside the park are available in such nearby communities as Florida City, Homestead, and Everglades City. Please consider using local facilities to decrease visitor impact on this fragile park.

Campgrounds

Campgrounds are open year-round. Reservations can be made by contacting the National Park Reservation Service at 800-365-CAMP. From November to May, the limit of stay is 14 days; otherwise, it is 30 days. From April through November, the park staff strongly discourages camping at Flamingo because of mosquitoes.

Backcountry Camping

Backcountry camping is allowed year-round throughout much of the park on a first-come, first-served basis. However, the park staff discourages backcountry camping from April through November because of mosquitoes. Free permits are required and can be obtained at vis-

▲ *Everglades National Park, Florida*

itor centers. In watery areas, designated camp-sites are on wooden platforms called "chickees."

FLORA AND FAUNA (Partial Listings)

Mammals: whitetail deer, the very rare Florida panther (mountain lion), bobcat, gray and red foxes, mink, river otter, longtail weasel, muskrat, raccoon, striped skunk, Virginia opossum, marsh rabbit, eastern cottontail, gray and fox squirrels, armadillo, manatee, bottle-nosed dolphin, and common pilot whale.

Birds: white and brown pelicans, anhinga, herons (great blue, white phase of great blue, little blue, tricolored, and green-backed), black-crowned and yellow-crowned night-herons, egrets (great, snowy, and cattle), white

ruddy turnstone, sandpipers (spotted, western, least, and pectoral), dunlin, short-billed dowitcher, gulls (laughing, ring-billed, and herring), terns (Caspian, royal, Forster's, and least), black skimmer, white-crowned pigeon, mourning dove, yellow-billed and mangrove cuckoos, smooth-billed ani, eastern screech and barred owls, nighthawk, chuck-will's-widow, ruby-throated hummingbird, belted kingfisher, red-bellied and pileated woodpeckers, flicker, eastern phoebe, great crested flycatcher, eastern and gray kingbirds, purple martin, tree and barn swallows, blue jay, crow, Carolina and house wrens, blue-gray gnatcatcher, catbird, mockingbird, vireos (white-eyed, red-eyed, and black-whiskered), warblers (northern parula, yellow, Cape May, black-throated blue, yellow-rumped, yellow-throated, pine, prairie, palm, and black-and-white), American redstart, common yellowthroat, ovenbird, northern and Louisiana water-thrushes, cardinal, indigo and painted buntings, rufous-sided towhee, sparrows (savannah, Cape Sable seaside, and swamp), bobolink, red-winged blackbird, eastern meadowlark, boat-tailed and common grackles, Baltimore oriole, and American goldfinch.

Reptiles and Amphibians: American alligator, American crocodile, turtles (Florida soft-shelled, Florida snapping, striped mud, and Florida red-bellied), diamondback terrapin, green and loggerhead sea turtles, green anole, frogs (green tree, southern leopard, and pig), 22 species of nonpoisonous snakes, including corn, scarlet, Everglades racer, ringneck, Everglades rat, mud, Florida king, green water, southern water, brown water, South Florida swamp, garter, and indigo, as well as four poisonous varieties—eastern coral snake, cottonmouth (water moccasin), and eastern diamondback and dusky pygmy rattlesnakes.

Marine Life: brain coral, sponges, starfish, spiny lobster, shrimp, crayfish, crabs (fiddler, blue, and stone), coon oyster, Florida gar, largemouth bass, barracuda, snapper, dolphin, and shark.

Insects: butterflies (swallowtail, sulphur, and black-and-yellow-banded zebra), dragonflies, and mosquitoes.

Trees, Shrubs, Flowers, Sedges, and Ferns: slash pine, bald and dwarf cypresses,

and glossy ibises, roseate spoonbill, wood stork, fulvous whistling-duck, mottled duck, pintail, northern shoveler, American wigeon, ring-necked duck, lesser scaup, red-breasted merganser, ruddy duck, black and turkey vultures, osprey, American swallow-tailed and snail kites, bald eagle, red-shouldered hawk, kestrel, bobwhite, rails (clapper, king, and sora), purple gallinule, common moorhen, coot, limpkin, black-bellied plover, killdeer, avocet, greater and lesser yellowlegs, willet, marbled godwit,

canella (cinnamon bark), Florida strangler-fig, live oak, Jamaica and bay-leaved capers, saffron plum, false-mastic, willow bustic, satinleaf, wild-dilly, joewood, marbleberry, Florida rapanea, myrtle laurelcherry, cocoplum, Bahama lysiloma, leadtree, eastern coral bean, pale lidflower, myrtle-of-the-river, a number of eugenias, mangroves (red, button, white, and black), tallowwood (hog plum), gulf graytwig (whitewood), Florida mayten, Florida crossopetalum, West Indies falsebox, tawnberry holly, oysterwood, manchineel, Cuban colubrina (soldierwood), wingleaf soapberry, gumbo-limbo, Florida poison tree, torchwood, lime and Biscayne prickly ashes, West Indies mahogany, holywood lignumvitae, key byrsonium, geiger-tree, Bahama strongbark, Florida fiddlewood, black calabash, common buttonbush, seven-year apple, roughleaf and Everglades velvetseeds, scarletbush, aloe yucca (Spanish bayonet), palms (Florida royal, Everglades, paurotis, and Florida silver), cabbage and saw palmettos, brittle and Florida thatch palms, swamp lily, alligator flag, coontie, glades lobelia, horned bladderwort, spatterdock, morning glory, sabatia marsh pink, night-blooming epidendrum, small catopsis, box briar, moonvine, nicker bean, prickly pear cactus, Jamaica sawgrass, the exotic water hyacinth, Boston and strap ferns, common and other bromeliads ("air-plants"), and more than 100 species of orchids, including clamshell, ghost, mule-ear, and vanilla.

NEARBY POINTS OF INTEREST

The area around the park offers other fascinating natural and cultural attractions that can be enjoyed as day trips or overnight excursions. Big Cypress National Preserve adjoins the park to the northwest. The J. N. "Ding" Darling National Wildlife Refuge and the National Audubon Society's Corkscrew Swamp Sanctuary are to the northwest, within 100 miles. Biscayne National Park is to the east, and Hobe Sound and Loxahatchee national wildlife refuges are to the northeast. Dry Tortugas National Park, including Fort Jefferson, lies about 180 miles southwest in the Gulf of Mexico and is accessible by boat or plane.

GREAT SMOKY MOUNTAINS NATIONAL PARK

▲ Red berries on mountain ash

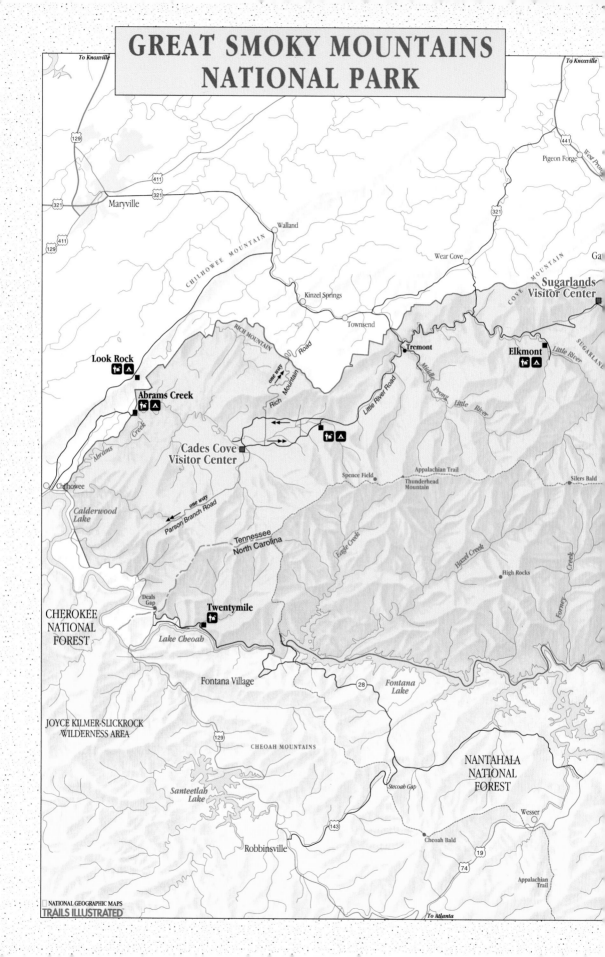

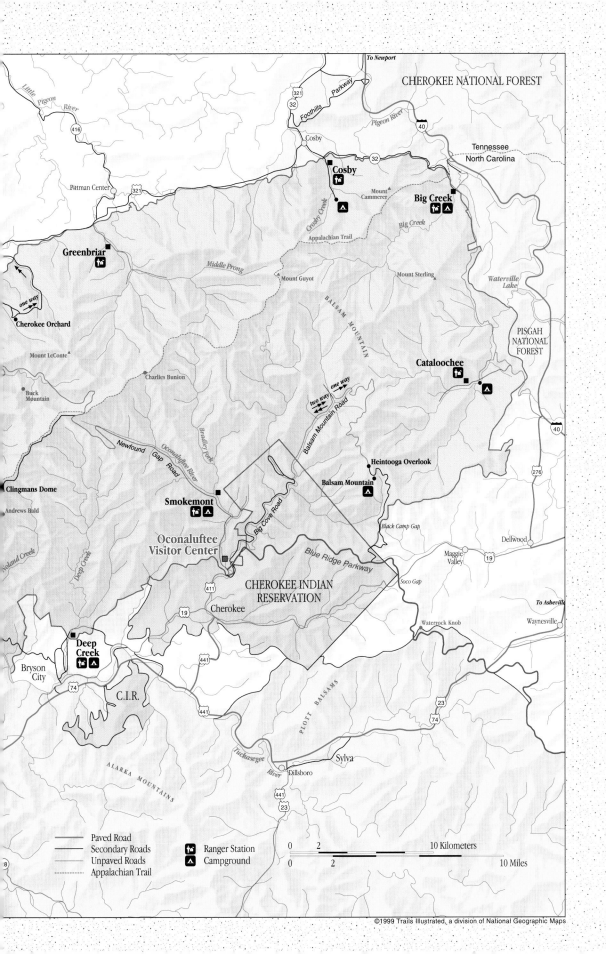

To Newport

CHEROKEE NATIONAL FOREST

Foothills Parkway

Pigeon River

Tennessee
North Carolina

Cosby

Cosby

Mount Cammerer

Big Creek

Big Creek

Pittman Center

Crosby Creek

Appalachian Trail

Greenbriar

Middle Prong

Mount Guyot

Mount Sterling

Waterville Lake

PISGAH NATIONAL FOREST

one way

Cherokee Orchard

BALSAM MOUNTAIN

Mount LeConte

Charlies Bunion

Bradley Fork

Cataloochee

one way
two way
Balsam Mountain Road

Buck Mountain

Newfound Gap Road

Oconaluftee River

Heintooga Overlook

Clingmans Dome

Balsam Mountain

Andrews Bald

Smokemont

Big Cove Road

Black Camp Gap

Dellwood

Noland Creek

Oconaluftee
Visitor Center

Blue Ridge Parkway

Maggie Valley

Deep Creek

CHEROKEE INDIAN
RESERVATION

Soco Gap

To Asheville

Cherokee

Waynesville

Deep Creek

Waterrock Knob

Bryson
City

C.I.R.

PLOTT BALSAMS

ALARKA MOUNTAINS

Tuckasegee River

Sylva

Dillsboro

Paved Road
Secondary Roads
Unpaved Roads
Appalachian Trail

Ranger Station
Campground

0   2   10 Kilometers

0   2   10 Miles

8

©1999 Trails Illustrated, a division of National Geographic Maps

Great Smoky Mountains National Park

**107 Park Headquarters Road
Gatlinburg, TN 37738
423-436-1200**

This 521,621-acre national park in western North Carolina and eastern Tennessee protects the scenically spectacular and ecologically rich Great Smoky Mountains—the climax of the southern Appalachian Mountains. Several mountains reach more than 6,000 feet above sea level, with Clingmans Dome the highest at 6,643 feet. Indeed, the Cherokee called this area "the Place of Blue Smoke" because of the bluish misty haze that often envelopes the mountains and fills the valleys. The park also includes a magnificent temperate deciduous forest, with 130 varieties of trees, nearly 1,500 flowering plants, 70 kinds of mammals, and more than 200 species of birds. Superb panoramic views, plunging waterfalls and cascades, rushing streams, hidden valleys, and coves all contribute to the wonder of this amazing land. The park was established in 1930, named a Biosphere Reserve in 1976, and designated a World Heritage Site in 1983.

OUTSTANDING FEATURES

Among the many outstanding features of the park are the following: **Newfound Gap**, the center of the park, offering excellent views from 5,048 feet; **Charlies Bunion**, a rocky knob from which hikers may enjoy one of the park's most spectacular panoramas; **Alum Cave Bluffs**, 100-foot-high cliffs that were the site of a 19th-century alum mine and a source of saltpeter for Civil War gunpowder; **Ramsay Cascades**, the park's highest waterfall, cascading 100 feet; **Rainbow Falls**, a beautiful 80-foot waterfall; **Abrams Falls**, a spectacular 20-foot waterfall; **Roaring Fork**, a 150-year-old village with log cabins and a cemetery; **Chimney Tops**, sheer pinnacles formed by the buckling of the earth; **Clingmans Dome**, at 6,643 feet above sea level, the highest point in the Smokies, reachable by road and an observation ramp; **Mount LeConte**, a 6,593-foot-high peak that is popular for viewing sunrises and sunsets; **Cades Cove**, an isolated valley settled in 1818 with log cabins, churches, an operating mill, and other buildings; and **Cataloochee Valley**, a less-visited valley with farmhouses, barns, a schoolhouse, and a church.

PRACTICAL INFORMATION

When to Go

The park is open year-round. Wildflowers and migrating birds abound in late April and early May. During June and July, rhododendrons bloom in spectacular profusion. Autumn's pageantry of color usually peaks at mid- to late October, when cool, clear days offer great hiking. Tourism is generally heaviest in summer and autumn.

How to Get There

By Car: U.S. Route 441 (Newfound Gap Road) runs through the park between Gatlinburg, Tennessee, and Cherokee, North Carolina.

By Air: McGhee-Tyson Airport is between Knoxville and Alcoa, Tennessee. Asheville Airport is about 60 miles east of the park, and Pigeon Forge Aviation Center is about 12 miles north in Sevierville, Tennessee.

By Train: Amtrak (800-872-7245) has stops in Charlotte, North Carolina. Great Smoky Mountains Railway (800-872-4681) runs from Bryson City, North Carolina.

By Bus: Greyhound Lines (800-231-2222) has stops in Sevierville, Tennessee. Shuttle service is available from McGhee-Tyson Airport to Gatlinburg, Tennessee.

Fees and Permits

There is no entrance fee. Backcountry use requires free permits, available at visitor centers and ranger stations. State fishing permits, locally available, are required for fishing in both Tennessee and North Carolina.

Visitor and Welcome Centers

Sugarlands Visitor Center: open daily year-round. Interpretive exhibits, programs, and publications.

Cades Cove Visitor Center: open daily from mid-April through October. Interpretive exhibits on cultural history, demonstrations, and schedules of events.

Oconaluftee Visitor Center: open daily year-round. Interpretive exhibits and publications.

Gatlinburg Welcome Center: lodging reservation system, information, exhibits, and publications.

Facilities

Cades Cove Campground has a campstore with limited picnic and camping supplies. Fuel and repair services are available in Gatlinburg and Townsend, Tennessee, and Cherokee, North Carolina.

Handicapped Accessibility

Sugarlands and Oconaluftee visitor centers and restrooms at Cades Cove, Chimney Tops, Cosby, and Mingus Mill are wheelchair-accessible. Park-orientation audiotapes and slide presentations are available at Sugarlands Visitor Center. Picnic areas at Chimney Tops and Cosby are accessible. Trails near Oconaluftee, Cades Cove, and Sugarlands are routes best suited for wheelchairs. Cataloochee and Big Creek campgrounds have level sites, and reservations can be made for sites near accessible restrooms at Cades Cove, Elkmont, and Smokemont from May through October by calling the National Park Reservation Service at 800-365-CAMP. Contact park headquarters for detailed information on accessibility.

Medical Services

First aid is available in the park. Hospitals, clinics, and other medical services are available in Gatlinburg, Pigeon Forge, and Sevierville, Tennessee, and Cherokee and Bryson City, North Carolina.

Pets

Pets must be leashed or otherwise physically restrained at all times.

Climate

Great Smoky Mountains' climate varies greatly depending on exposure and elevation. Along ridge tops, cooler temperatures and higher precipitation are common. In winter, precipitation falls as rain in the valleys and as snow or rain on the ridges. Average daily temperature range in Fahrenheit and average daily precipitation for lower elevation areas are as follows:

	AVERAGE DAILY	
Month	**Temperature F**	**Precipitation**
January	25-48°	4.5 inches
February	26-51°	4.2 inches
March	33-60°	5.6 inches
April	42-70°	4.5 inches
May	48-76°	4.4 inches
June	56-82°	4.6 inches
July	60-84°	5.1 inches
August	59-84°	4.5 inches
September	53-78°	3.7 inches
October	41-70°	3.0 inches
November	32-59°	3.7 inches
December	27-51°	4.2 inches

Worship Services

Nondenominational Christian worship services, sponsored by "A Christian Ministry in the National Parks," are held on Sundays at 10 a.m. and 6 p.m. in the amphitheaters at Smokemont, Cades Cove, Elkmont, and Deep Creek campgrounds and at 9 a.m. at Cosby Campground.

Safety and Regulations

For your safety and enjoyment and for the protection of the park, please follow these regulations and suggestions:

▲ *Appalachian Trail, Great Smoky Mountains National Park, Tennessee-North Carolina border*

- Remember that it is unlawful to feed, disturb, capture, trap, or hunt wildlife.

- Firearms are strictly forbidden.

- Open fires are prohibited except at designated sites. Use only dead and downed wood.

- Use of tents at shelters is prohibited.

- Campers should keep all food in bear-proof containers, in vehicle trunks, or suspended at least ten feet off the ground and four feet from the nearest limb or tree trunk.

- Motorized vehicles, bicycles, and pets are prohibited in the backcountry.

- The National Park Service urges that backcountry hikers leave their planned itinerary with others and be equipped with appropriate clothing and gear. Hikers are advised to stay on trails, keep safely back from hazardous cliff edges, watch that children avoid hazardous situations, and be careful around fast-flowing streams, waterfalls, and wet, slippery rock surfaces.

Options include free ranger-led activities such as interpretive walks and talks, evening campfire programs, slide shows, films, and children's programs. Other activities include scenic drives, field seminars and workshops, hiking, birdwatching, picnicking, camping, bicycling, guided tours, horseback riding, fishing, living-history demonstrations, and special cultural events, such as quilt shows, storytelling, and apple-butter making. Winter activities include cross-country skiing, sledding, and tobogganing. Further information is provided in the park's newspaper, *Smokies Trip Planner*.

Tours

Smoky Mountain Tours (800-962-0448) and Mountain Tours (423-453-0864) both offer bus tours through the park and operate from Gatlinburg.

Smoky Mountains Audio Tour: The Newfound Gap Road, two 60-minute cassette tapes, serve as a personal tour guide on the park's Newfound Gap Road. The tape includes explanations of landmarks, interviews with rangers and scientists, and Cherokee legends. The tape is available for $9.95 plus shipping from the Great Smoky Mountains Natural History Association, 115 Park Headquarters Road, Gatlinburg, TN 37738; 423-436-7318.

Hiking Trails

The park has more than 800 miles of trails, suitable for all levels of physical ability. The National Park Service asks hikers to observe minimum-impact hiking practices, stay on trails, hike with others, leave detailed plans with a ranger, be alert for bears, and treat all water. *Quiet Walkways* are easy, one-fourth-mile paths into what signs call "a little bit of the world as it once was." Samples of trails at varying degrees of difficulty are outlined below; trail maps are available from visitor centers or bookstores. The Great Smoky Mountains Natural History Association publishes a comprehensive guide to the official trails of the park titled *Hiking Trails of the Smokies*. It is available by contacting the association at 115 Park Headquarters Road, Gatlinburg, TN 37738; 615-436-7318.

Trails include the following: **Clingmans Dome Trail**, an easy half-mile paved path on the park's highest mountain, beginning at the end of the Clingmans Dome Road (closed in winter) and, on clear days, affording grand panoramas; **Indian Creek Falls Trail**, an easy, one-mile route beginning at the trailhead at the end of Deep Creek Road and leading to this impressive, 60-foot waterfall; **Laurel Falls Trail**, an easy and very popular, 1.25-mile, paved path beginning at Laurel Falls parking area on Little River Road and leading through a pine and oak forest with lots of rhododendrons to this lovely waterfall; **Balsam Mountain Trail**, an easy, 1.5-mile loop route beginning at the Balsam Mountain Campground and leading through a beautiful forest; **Hen Wallow Falls Trail**, a moderate, two-mile route beginning at the trailhead on road to Cosby Campground and leading to both the top and bottom of this picturesque waterfall; **Chimney Tops Trail**, a strenuous, two-mile route beginning at the trailhead on the Newfound Gap Road and winding through old-growth forest to the Chimney Tops pinnacles; **Abrams Falls Trail**, an easy 2.5-mile route beginning at Abrams Falls parking area on the Cades Cove Loop Road and leading to this spectacular 20-foot-high waterfall; **Rainbow Falls Trail**, a moderate 3.5-mile route beginning at Cherokee Orchard and leading to this beautiful 80-foot waterfall; **Alum Cave Bluffs Trail**, an easy then difficult, 5.5-mile route beginning at Newfound Gap Road between Newfound Gap and Chimney Tops and leading to Arch Rock, Alum Cave Bluffs (100-foot-high cliffs), and Mount LeConte; the cliff-skirting stretch of this trail, where hikers hold on to a cable, should be attempted only in favorable weather and by visitors in good health using great care; **Ramsay Cascades Trail**, a strenuous, four-mile route beginning at the trailhead at the end of the Greenbrier Cove Road and leading through old-growth deciduous forest to this 100-foot-high waterfall—the park's highest; **Boulevard Trail**, a moderate to strenuous, 16-mile route beginning along the Appalachian Trail from Newfound Gap and leading to the summit of Mount LeConte; and **Appalachian Trail**, a 70-mile stretch of the 2,100-mile-long trail that runs from Maine to Georgia, accessed at Newfound Gap,

Clingmans Dome near the end of State Highway 32 at Fontana Dam, and near Exit 451 on I-40.

Fishing

Fishing is permitted from sunrise to sunset with a valid Tennessee or North Carolina fishing license, available at sporting goods stores and at the chamber of commerce in Gatlinburg. Only single-hook artificial lures are allowed; fishing with bait is prohibited. Trout stamps are not required. Available fish are smallmouth bass, rock bass, rainbow trout, and brown trout. All state regulations apply, and a list is available at visitor centers. Popular fishing spots are Abram Creek below Cades Cove, Big Creek near Interstate 40 at the northeastern end of the park, Little River near Elkmont Campground, and Fontana Lake.

Bicycling

Roads are steep and narrow, and bicycles are prohibited on trails. Cades Cove and Cataloochee Valley, however, have excellent biking areas. The 11-mile loop road around Cades Cove is available for bicycling and closed to motorized vehicles from sunrise to 10 a.m., Saturdays and Wednesdays, from early May to mid-September. Rental bikes are available at the Cades Cove Campground store.

Horseback Riding

Horse rentals are available by the hour or half-day from stables at Cades Cove (423-448-6286) and Smokemont (704-497-2373) campgrounds; from McCarter's Riding Stables (423-436-5354); and from Smoky Mountains Riding Stables (423-436-5634). Visitors with their own horses should contact the park for an official trail map and guide containing regulations, trails, and camping information for horse use.

Scenic Drives

In addition to the main, through-park highway (U.S. Route 441) crossing Newfound Gap, other scenic drives include the following: **Clingmans Dome Road**, a seven-mile, paved spur road (closed in winter) branching from U.S. Route 441 and leading to the park's highest mountain, from which on clear days there are grand panoramas; **Little River Road**, an 18-mile, paved road beginning at Sugarlands Visitor Center and affording views of Little River and waterfalls; **Cades Cove Loop Road**, an 11-mile, one-way loop road through this scenic and historic valley (note: only bicycles and foot traffic are permitted on this road from sunrise to 10 a.m. on Saturdays and Wednesdays from early May to mid-September); and **Roaring Fork Motor Nature Trail**, a narrow, paved, one-way, six-mile road beginning and ending in Gatlinburg and affording views of lush forest, dashing streams, and plunging waterfalls.

OVERNIGHT STAYS

Overnight Lodging and Dining

LeConte Lodge, open from mid-March to mid-November and accessible only by hiking to the summit of Mount LeConte, provides cabins (shared bathrooms and no electricity) and meals from mid-March to mid-November. Reservations are necessary and can be made through LeConte Lodge, 250 Apple Valley Road, Sevierville, TN 37862; 423-429-5704.

Lodging Outside the Park

Lodging and dining facilities are available in nearby communities, such as Gatlinburg, Pigeon Forge, Sevierville, and Townsend, Tennessee, and Bryson City and Cherokee, North Carolina.

Campgrounds

All campgrounds operate on a first-come, first-served basis unless otherwise noted. There are no trailer hookups at campgrounds. Camping at Cades Cove, Elkmont, and Smokemont between May 15 and November 1 requires reservations through the National Park Reservation Service (800-365-CAMP). Group camping requires reservations made through the same reservation service for Cades Cove, Elkmont, and Smokemont campgrounds or by calling park headquarters for other group campgrounds. Group campgrounds are for organized groups only, and each one has a

different group-size limit per site. The limit of stay between May 15 and November 1 is seven days; otherwise, it is 14 days.

Backcountry Camping

Backcountry camping is permitted throughout the park year-round. Reservations are required for shelters and restricted sites; contact the park's Backcountry Reservations office. A

▲ *Ledge Creek, Great Smoky Mountains National Park, North Carolina*

backcountry permit is also required. Camping parties may include up to eight people. Three-sided shelters are provided at 18 areas. The limit of stay for each backcountry site is three days, or one day in shelters. The total permitted length of stay in the backcountry is 14 days. The National Park Service urges campers to keep a clean, odor-free campsite and to store food high in trees or on poles provided to avoid attracting black bears. An official trail map and guide provides detailed backcountry information and regulations.

FLORA AND FAUNA (Partial Listings)

Mammals: black bear, whitetail deer, bobcat, the re-introduced red wolf, red and gray foxes, the re-introduced river otter, mink, long-tail weasel, beaver, muskrat, raccoon, spotted and striped skunks, woodchuck, opossum, eastern and New England cottontails, squirrels (gray, fox, flying, and red), eastern chipmunk, and the exotic European wild boar.

Birds: wood duck, great blue heron, wild turkey, ruffed grouse, bobwhite, hawks (red-tailed, red-shouldered, and broad-winged), black and turkey vultures, owls (barred, saw-whet, screech, and great horned), belted kingfisher, mourning dove, yellow-billed cuckoo, whip-poor-will, ruby-throated hummingbird, woodpeckers (pileated, red-bellied, downy, hairy, and red-cockaded), flicker, yellow-bellied sapsucker, eastern kingbird, great crested and Acadian flycatchers, eastern wood pewee, eastern phoebe, chimney swift, barn swallow, crow, raven, blue jay, Carolina and black-capped chickadees, tufted titmouse, white-breasted and red-breasted nuthatches, brown creeper, winter and Carolina wrens, golden-crowned kinglet, brown thrasher, catbird, mockingbird, robin, veery, Swainson's and wood thrushes, vireos (solitary, white-eyed, and red-eyed), warblers (yellow-rumped, Canada, black-throated green, black-and-white, black-throated blue, chestnut-sided, blackburnian, yellow, hooded, northern parula, worm-eating, and yellow-throated), American redstart, yellow-breasted chat, summer and scarlet tanagers, sparrows (white-throated, chipping, field, and song), rufous-sided towhee, dark-eyed junco, rose-breasted grosbeak, indigo bunting, cardinal, purple finch, and American goldfinch.

Reptiles and Amphibians: green frog, snakes (copperhead, five-lined, and northern water), timber rattlesnake, and 27 species of salamanders, including hellbender, pygmy, slimy, two-lined, Appalachian woodland, long-tailed, red-cheeked, and black-chinned red.

Trees, Shrubs, and Flowers: pines (eastern white, table mountain, Virginia, and pitch), red spruce, eastern and Carolina hemlocks, Fraser fir, cucumber tree, umbrella magnolia, tuliptree (yellow poplar), sassafras, sweetgum, witch hazel, hickories (mockernut, shagbark, and pignut), beech, oaks (white, chestnut, northern red, black, and scarlet), American hornbeam, sweet and yellow birches, American basswood, sourwood, persimmon, Carolina silverbell, black and pin cherries, mountain ash, serviceberry, eastern redbud, black locust, flowering dogwood, black tupelo, American holly, yellow buckeye, maples (mountain, striped, red, and sugar), green and white ashes, the spectacular Catawba rhododendron (purple or rosy-purple flowers), Carolina or dwarf rhododendron (reddish-purple flowers), rosebay rhododendron (white or pinkish-white flowers), mountain laurel, flame azalea, shadbush, hobblebush, blueberry, blue-crested dwarf iris, skunk cabbage, bluet, spring beauty, fire-pink, bloodroot, Mayapple, jack-in-the-pulpit, foamflower, trout-lily, 32 varieties of violets, Solomon's-seal, false Solomon's-seal, Dutchman's-breeches, columbine, eight species of trilliums, galax, cardinal flower, nearly 30 species of orchids, including pink and yellow lady's-slippers, coneflower, goldenrods, and asters.

NEARBY POINTS OF INTEREST

The area surrounding this park offers many significant natural and historical attractions that can be enjoyed as day trips or overnight excursions. The Blue Ridge Parkway extends from Great Smoky Mountains National Park to Shenandoah National Park in Virginia. Cherokee and Pisgah national forests adjoin the park in Tennessee; and Nantahala National Forests adjoins the park in North Carolina. Andrew Johnson National Historic Site is to northeast in Tennessee. Big South Fork National River and Recreation Area is to the northwest in Tennessee.

Hot Springs National Park

▲ *Azaleas in bloom*

Hot Springs National Park

P.O. Box 1860
Hot Springs, AR 71902-1860
501-623-1433

This 5,549-acre national park in the Zig Zag Mountains of central Arkansas features a historic 19th-century health spa, 47 hot springs, and an area of forested hills that provides a diversity of flora and fauna and miles of hiking trails. The thermal waters are heated at great depths, roughly 4,000 to 8,000 feet below the earth's surface; then, hydrostatic pressure forces the water to the surface through cracks and faults in the bedrock. The park's springs pour forth roughly 850,000 gallons at 143 degrees Fahrenheit on an average day. For the past 10,000 years, people have come to bathe, drink, heal, and relax in these therapeutic mineral waters. By the early 20th century, when the bathhouses at Hot Springs were at the peak of their popularity, people traveled from all across the country for treatment of such ailments as arthritis and rheumatism. The springs, which produce naturally sterile water, have been used not only to help prevent the spread of certain diseases, but even to hold NASA's moon rocks while they were studied for evidence of life. Hot Springs Reservation was set aside in 1832, dedicated as a public park in 1880, and established as a national park in 1921.

OUTSTANDING FEATURES

Among the many outstanding features of the park are the following: **Hot Springs Mountain**, the peak from which the waters flow; **Hot Springs Mountain Observation Tower**, which affords a superb view of the city of Hot Springs and its surrounding mountains; **Bathhouse Row**, monumental bathhouses dating from the late 19th and early 20th centuries, which were restored in the 1980s; **Gulpha Gorge**, a rich and rugged woodland; and **DeSoto Rock**, a huge boulder that commemorates both the Indians who resided

in the general area of the park and explorer Hernando De Soto.

PRACTICAL INFORMATION

When to Go

The park is open year-round. The climate is usually favorable with mild, short winters. Summers are hot; crowds peak in July. Autumn is ideal, featuring cooler temperatures and spectacular colors of foliage on the surrounding mountains.

How to Get There

By Car: From Little Rock, drive southwest 25 miles on I-30 and west 30 miles on U.S. Route 70. From Texarkana, drive northeast 78 miles on I-30 and north 30 miles on State Route 7.

By Air: Hot Springs Municipal Airport (501-623-8233) and Adams Field (501-372-3439) are served by most major airlines.

By Train: Amtrak (800-872-7245) has stops in Little Rock, with Thruway Bus Connection to Hot Springs.

By Bus: Greyhound Lines (800-231-2222) has stops in Hot Springs. All Around Arkansas Tours (800-648-8199) runs charters. City bus service is also available.

Fees and Permits

Fees are charged at commercially operated bathhouses.

Visitor Center

Fordyce Bathhouse Visitor Center: open daily, except Thanksgiving, Christmas, and New Year's Day. Interpretive exhibits, audiovisual programs, tours, schedules, and publications.

Facilities

Available are picnic areas and a campground.

Handicapped Accessibility

The visitor center, parts of Bathhouse Row, and Thermal Features trails are wheelchair-accessible. A bulletin provides detailed information on accessibility.

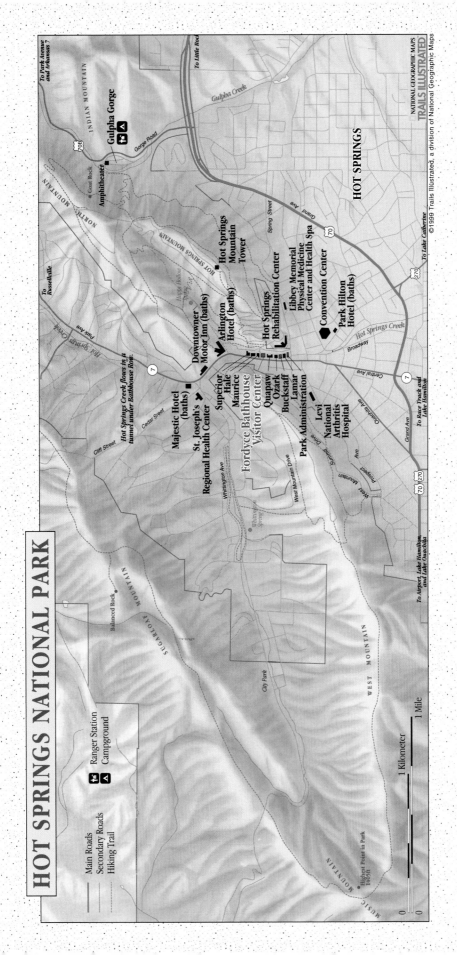

HOT SPRINGS NATIONAL PARK

Main Roads
Secondary Roads
Hiking Trail

Ranger Station
Campground

1 Mile
1 Kilometer

NATIONAL GEOGRAPHIC MAPS
TRAILS ILLUSTRATED
©1999 Trails Illustrated, a division of National Geographic Maps

To Park Avenue
and Arkansas 7

INDIAN MOUNTAIN

Gulpha Creek

Gulpha Gorge

To Little Rock

Gorge Road

705

Goat Rock

NORTH MOUNTAIN

Amphitheater

HOT SPRINGS MOUNTAIN

Hot Springs
Mountain Tower

HOT SPRINGS

Spring Street

Grand Ave

To Lake Catherine

70

Happy Hollow Springs

To Russellville

Park Ave

Arlington
Hotel (baths)

Downtowner
Motor Inn (baths)

Hot Springs
Rehabilitation Center

Libbey Memorial
Physical Medicine
Center and Health Spa

Convention Center

Park Hilton
Hotel (baths)

Hot Springs Creek

Broadway

270

7

Hot Springs Creek flows in a
tunnel under Bathhouse Row.

Cedar Street

Majestic Hotel
(baths)

St. Joseph's
Regional Health Center

Cliff Street

Superior
Hale
Maurice
Fordyce Bathhouse
Visitor Center
Quapaw
Ozark
Buckstaff
Lamar
Park Administration

Levi
National
Arthritis
Hospital

Central Ave

Ouachita Ave

To Race Track and
Lake Hamilton

7

Whittington Ave

West Mountain Drive

Whittington
Spring

Sunset Drive

Prospect Ave

West Mountain

Grand Ave

70 270

To Airport, Lake Hamilton,
and Lake Ouachita

SUGARLOAF MOUNTAIN

Balanced Rock

City Park

WEST MOUNTAIN

MUSIC MOUNTAIN

Highest Point in Park
1405 ft

0

0

Medical Services

The city of Hot Springs has two hospitals and other medical facilities.

Pets

Pets must be leashed or otherwise physically restrained at all times.

Safety and Regulations

For your safety and enjoyment and for the protection of the park, please follow these regulations and suggestions:

- Drive carefully. The scenic roads are steep and curving, and designed for slow sightseeing travel.

- The hiking trails traverse uneven terrain; appropriate footgear is advised.

- Remember that feeding, disturbing, capturing, or hunting wildlife is prohibited. Damaging or removing trees, plants, or other natural objects is also not allowed.

- Visitors are cautioned to be alert for ticks, snakes, and poison ivy.

- Motor vehicles and bicycles are not permitted on sidewalks and trails.

- Fires are permitted only in designated fireplaces.

ACTIVITIES

Options include thermal water use (baths, whirlpools, steam cabinets, hot packs, massages), hiking, tours, guided walks and talks, campfire programs, picnicking, camping, audiovisual and interpretive exhibits, and horseback riding. Further information is available in the park's newspaper, *Hot Springs Pipeline*.

Trails

Among the park's numerous trails are the following: **Grand Promenade**, an easy half-mile, landscaped route designated as a national recreation trail and providing a pleasant, red-and-yellow brick walk from the bathhouse area to the mountains; **Peak Trail**, a moderately strenuous, half-mile, scenic route beginning

51

▲ *Music Room, Fordyce Bathhouse, Hot Springs National Park, Arkansas*

midway along the Promenade and climbing to the summit of Hot Springs Mountain, where Mountain Tower is located and where there are a picnic area and related facilities; **Gulpha Gorge Trail**, a moderately strenuous .8-mile route beginning at Gulpha Gorge Campground, crossing Gulpha Creek, leading along the steep sides of the gorge, and ending at North Mountain Road (near a trail shelter); **Dead Chief Trail**, a partly strenuous, 1.4-mile route between Fordyce Bathhouse Visitor Center and Gulpha Gorge Campground; **Goat Rock Trail**, a moderate 1.1-mile route between Gulpha Gorge Trail and North Mountain Overlook and leading beneath Goat Rock; **Dogwood Trail**, a walk containing two loops—a .7-mile lower loop and a one-mile upper loop on North Mountain and providing beautiful scenes of spring blossoming of dogwood trees; and **West Mountain Trail**, a moderate, 1.2-mile loop beginning and ending at a shelter on the West Mountain Summit Drive.

OVERNIGHT STAYS

Lodging and Dining

There are no lodging or dining facilities within the park, but there are many in the city of Hot Springs and at nearby lakes. Further information is available by contacting the Hot Springs Advertising and Promotion Commission at 800-SPA-CITY.

Campground

Gulpha Gorge Campground is open year-round on a first-come, first-served basis with a 14-day limit. Fires are permitted only in provided grills or in camp stoves. No electrical power or water is available at individual campsites.

FLORA AND FAUNA (Partial Listings)

Mammals: whitetail deer, gray and red foxes, raccoon, spotted and striped skunks, woodchuck, opossum, armadillo, eastern cottontail, squirrels

(gray, fox, and flying), and eastern chipmunk.

Birds: wild turkey, yellow-billed cuckoo, owls (great horned, barred, and eastern screech), chimney swift, ruby-throated hummingbird, woodpeckers (red-bellied, downy, hairy, and pileated), flicker, eastern kingbird, great crested and Acadian flycatchers, eastern wood pewee, eastern phoebe, blue jay, crow, tufted titmouse, Carolina chickadee, brown creeper, white-breasted nuthatch, Carolina wren, wood thrush, robin, catbird, mockingbird, brown thrasher, white-eyed and warbling vireos, warblers (black-and-white, pine, and yellow), American redstart, Louisiana waterthrush, cardinal, indigo bunting, rufous-sided towhee, sparrows (song, chipping, and white-throated), Baltimore oriole, summer tanager, and American goldfinch.

Trees, Shrubs, Flowers, and Ferns: shortleaf pine, the introduced southern magnolia, umbrella magnolia, sassafras, sweetgum, witch hazel, hickories, Allegheny chinkapin, oaks (white, post, southern red, and black), American hornbeam (musclewood), hazel alder, Carolina silverbell, eastern redbud, flowering dogwood, black tupelo, American holly, red buckeye, red maple, Mayapple, crested iris, bluet, partridgeberry, pussytoes, yellow lousewort, wood sorrel, wild phlox, bird's-foot violet, cardinal flower, shooting star, fire pink, black-eyed Susan, and ebony spleenwort, bracken, Christmas, and resurrection ferns.

NEARBY POINTS OF INTEREST

The area surrounding this park offers other fascinating natural and cultural attractions that can be enjoyed as day trips or overnight excursions. The entrance to Ouachita National Forest is about five miles to the east. Ozark National Forest and Holla Bend National Wildlife Refuge are both located north of Hot Springs. Buffalo National River is about 100 miles to the north. Other National Park System units in Arkansas are Arkansas Post National Memorial in Gillett; Fort Smith National Historic Site in Fort Smith (also in Oklahoma); and Pea Ridge National Military Park in Pea Ridge.

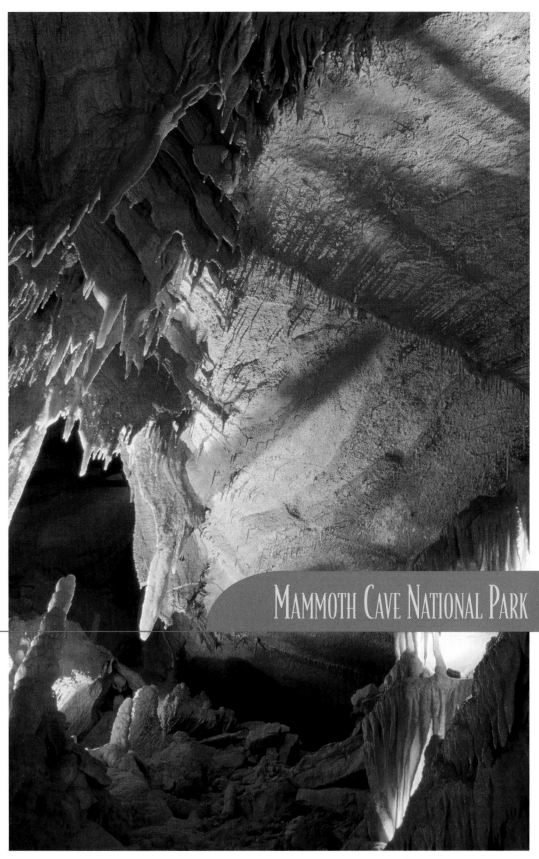

Mammoth Cave National Park

▲ *Limestone formations, Drapery Room*

Mammoth Cave National Park

**Mammoth Cave, KY 42259
502-758-2328**

This 52,830-acre national park in southwest Kentucky protects nearly 300 caves that comprise the most diverse and by far the largest-known cavern system in the world. Approximately 350 miles of underground passageways at five different levels have been explored so far, and "speleologists" are continuing to make new discoveries. Of the hundreds of cave entrances into the limestone labyrinth, there are five by which visitors enter on guided tours. While much of the cave system is dry and thus mostly lacking the stalagmites and stalactites of caves elsewhere, visitors can see a few magnificent displays of flowstone and dripstone formations and intricate gypsum crystals in the shapes of flowers, angel-hair, and needles. In certain areas, rivers, waterfalls, and lakes, and underground streams have carved towering columns, cavernous pits and domes, long tubular passageways, and narrow canyons. At the lowest cave level, such underground rivers as the River Styx and Echo River continue to flow and carve subterranean passages. Animal life inside the cave includes rare sightless cavefish, crayfish, cave shrimp, cave snails, spiders, millipedes, and beetles. Other creatures, including salamanders and a dozen species of bats, are among the more than 200 species of fauna.

The surface of the park consists of richly forested hills, through which meander the Green and Nolin rivers. Nearly 70 miles of hiking trails wind throughout the park, providing opportunities to see a diversity of wildlife, including approximately 40 kinds of mammals, 200 species of birds, and 1,000 varieties of flowering plants (including 84 species of trees). Ferries cross the Green River at two places, and scenic river cruises are offered from April through October. The park was established in 1941 and was designated a World Heritage Site in 1981 and a Biosphere Reserve in 1990.

OUTSTANDING FEATURES

Among the many outstanding features of the park are the following: **Drapery Room**, an area in the Frozen Niagara section, containing exquisite displays of flowstone, stalactites, stalagmites, draperies, and columns, such as in the Lion's Cage; **Frozen Niagara**, a magnificent, 75-foot-high cascade of travertine flowstone; **Ruins of Karnack**, huge water-carved columns in 192-foot-high Mammoth Dome, which was created by water dripping through a sinkhole above; **Moonlight Dome**, a dome embellished with flowstone formations and containing a pond at the bottom of its pit; **Chief City**, the largest room in Mammoth Cave; and the **Green River,** one of the most biologically diverse rivers in North America.

PRACTICAL INFORMATION

When to Go

The park is open year-round, and tours are given every day except Christmas. Reservations for cave tours are strongly recommended. Seasons do not affect the cave temperature, which remains at 54 degrees Fahrenheit, but there are more crowds and more tours during the summer. Above ground at the park, spring is beautiful with flowering trees and wildflowers, and autumn is spectacular with foliage colors.

How to Get There

By Car: From Louisville, take I-65 south 65 miles to Exit 53 at Cave City, then west on State Route 70 to the visitor center. From Nashville, take I-65 north to exit 48 at Park City and on to the visitor center.

By Air: There are airports in Nashville, Tennessee, and Louisville and Bowling Green, Kentucky.

By Bus: Greyhound Lines (800-231-2222) has stops in Cave City.

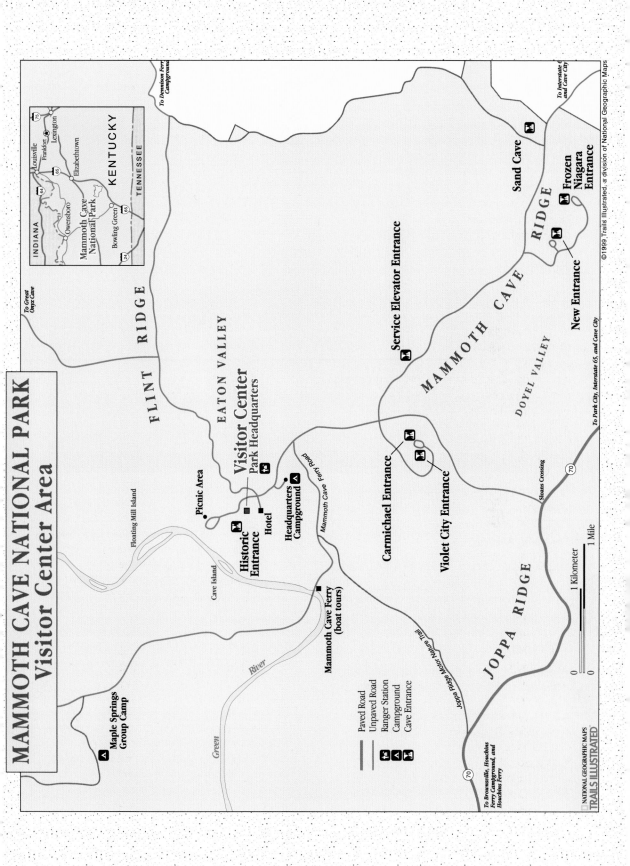

MAMMOTH CAVE NATIONAL PARK
Visitor Center Area

KENTUCKY

INDIANA

Louisville
Frankfort
Lexington
Elizabethtown
Owensboro
Bowling Green
Mammoth Cave National Park

TENNESSEE

To Great Onyx Cave

To Dennison Ferry Campground

To Interstate and Cave City

FLINT RIDGE

EATON VALLEY

Floating Mill Island

Maple Springs Group Camp

Green River

Cave Island

Mammoth Cave Ferry (boat tours)

Historic Entrance

Hotel

Headquarters Campground

Picnic Area

Visitor Center
Park Headquarters

Ferry Road

Mammoth Cave

Carmichael Entrance

Violet City Entrance

Service Elevator Entrance

MAMMOTH CAVE RIDGE

DOYEL VALLEY

Sand Cave

Frozen Niagara Entrance

New Entrance

Sloans Crossing

JOPPA RIDGE

Joppa Ridge Motor Nature Trail

To Brownsville, Houchins Ferry Campground, and Houchins Ferry

To Park City, Interstate 65, and Cave City

70

70

Paved Road
Unpaved Road
Ranger Station
Campground
Cave Entrance

NATIONAL GEOGRAPHIC MAPS
TRAILS ILLUSTRATED

0   1 Kilometer
0   1 Mile

©1999 Trails Illustrated, a division of National Geographic Maps

▲ *Green River, Mammoth Cave National Park, Kentucky*

Fees and Permits

There are no entrance fees to the park, but fees are charged for cave tours, camping, and boat trips. Free backcountry permits, available at the visitor center, are required.

Visitor Center

Mammoth Cave Visitor Center: open daily, except Christmas. Cave and boat tour reservations and tickets, information, interpretive exhibits, programs, publications, and backcountry permits.

Facilities

Available are picnic areas, campgrounds, amphitheater, lodging, restaurant, laundry (seasonal), service station, store, post office, hot showers (seasonal), and boat launches.

Handicapped Accessibility

The visitor center, Heritage Trail, Tour for the Mobility Impaired, Mammoth Cave Hotel, two campsites and rest rooms at Headquarters Campground, and the amphitheater are wheelchair-accessible. Call 502-758-2328 for detailed information on accessibility.

Medical Services

First aid is available at the visitor center. A hospital is located in Horse Cave, ten miles from the park.

Pets

The Mammoth Cave Hotel, adjacent to the visitor center, offers a pet kennel with fees by the hour or day. Only guide dogs are permitted in the cave. Pets left in parked vehicles may be removed by park personnel because temperatures inside may threaten the life of the pet. Pets must be leashed or otherwise physically restrained at all times.

Safety and Regulations

For your safety and enjoyment and for the protection of the park, please follow these regulations and suggestions:

- Visitors are advised to be alert for ticks, chiggers, copperhead snakes, timber rattlesnakes, and poison ivy.

- Remember that it is illegal to feed, disturb, capture, or hunt wildlife.

- Licenses are not required for fishing, but state regulations apply.

- On cave tours, children under six years of age must be accompanied by an adult, and strollers are not allowed. Some cave tours do not have restroom facilities. All tours are strenuous and require stooping and walking over rough, uneven terrain. Smoking is prohibited in the cave. Sturdy shoes or hiking boots are recommended; sandals or bare feet are not permitted. Cameras, video recorders, food and drink, and flashlights are permitted, but tripods are not allowed inside the cave. Visitors are reminded to use trash receptacles and not to litter the areas. Also, please use courtesy when shining flashlights and remember that they must be turned off during tour stops.

ACTIVITIES

Options include cave tours, scenic drives, hiking, ranger-led programs, boating, canoeing, boat cruises, bicycling, horseback riding, birdwatching, fishing, picnicking, camping, and occasional special events. Canoe and horse rentals are available at private concessions outside the park. Reservations for cave tours are especially important for the summer months and weekends. Advance reservations can be made by calling 800-967-2283. As cave touring is strenuous—some tour routes more than others—visitors with walking, heart, or respiratory difficulties are advised to consult with a park ranger. Scenic boat cruises on the Green River are offered from April through October, as river conditions permit. Tickets can be purchased at the visitor center; for informa-

tion, call 502-758-2243. Further information on park activities is available in the park's newspaper, *Mammoth Cave Guide*.

Hiking Trails

Trails include the following: **Heritage Trail**, an easy half-mile route beginning and ending just west of the hotel, affording a view at an overlook (an interpretive tape on this walk is available at the visitor center); **Cave Island Nature Trail**, an easy one-mile loop beginning and ending at the historic entrance of Mammoth Cave and winding through the forest; **Green River Bluffs Trail**, an easy one-mile route between the visitor center and the picnic area to the north of the historic entrance, leading along forested bluffs above the Green River; **Turnhole Bend Trail**, an easy half-mile loop beginning and ending at Turnhole parking area on State Route 70, leading along forested river bluffs, and affording views of three sinkholes; and **Echo River Trail**, a moderate, two-mile route winding south and passing the place where the Echo River emerges at a spring.

OVERNIGHT STAYS

Lodging and Dining

Mammoth Cave Hotel: open all year, offering hotel rooms and a restaurant. Rustic cabins are available from spring to autumn. For reservations, contact Mammoth Cave Hotel, Mammoth Cave, KY 42259; 502-758-2225.

Campgrounds

Three campgrounds are open in spring, summer, and autumn; reservations can be made by contacting the National Park Reservation Service at 800-967-CAVE. Two handicapped-accessible sites at Headquarters Campground (502-758-2251), located near accessible restrooms, are held until 6 p.m. each day during the summer for mobility-impaired campers. The group campground is open spring, summer, and autumn; reservations are required and can be made by calling park headquarters. Three sites are equipped to accommodate horses; eight horses are allowed per site.

Backcountry Camping

Backcountry camping is allowed year-round at designated sites on a first-come, first-served basis, as well as on river banks and islands. Free permits are required and can be obtained at the visitor center.

FLORA AND FAUNA (Partial Listings)

Mammals: whitetail deer, bobcat, gray and red foxes, mink, longtail weasel, muskrat, raccoon, spotted and striped skunks, beaver, woodchuck, opossum, eastern cottontail, gray and fox squirrels, and eastern chipmunk.

Birds: green-backed and great blue heron, Canada goose, mallard, wood duck, hawks (red-shouldered, broad-winged, and red-tailed), kestrel, bobwhite, wild turkey, mourning dove, owls (great horned, barred, and eastern screech), chimney swift, ruby-throated hummingbird, belted kingfisher, woodpeckers (red-bellied, red-headed, downy, hairy, and pileated), great crested and Acadian flycatchers, eastern wood pewee, eastern phoebe, blue jay, crow, tufted titmouse, Carolina chickadee, white-breasted nuthatch, Carolina wren, blue-gray gnatcatcher, eastern bluebird, wood thrush, robin, catbird, mockingbird, brown thrasher, white-eyed and red-eyed vireo, warblers (prothonotary, blue-winged, black-and-white, cerulean, yellow-throated, prairie, yellow, Kentucky, hooded, and worm-eating), ovenbird, Louisiana waterthrush, common yellowthroat, yellow-breasted chat, American redstart, cardinal, rufous-sided towhee, sparrows (song, chipping, and white-throated), dark-eyed junco, red-winged blackbird, Baltimore oriole, and scarlet and summer tanager.

Trees, Shrubs, and Flowers: pines (shortleaf, Virginia, and loblolly), eastern hemlock, eastern red cedar, umbrella magnolia, tuliptree (yellow poplar), sassafras, American sycamore, sweetgum, witch hazel, American elm, shagbark and other hickories, beech, white and black oaks, yellow birch, mountain laurel, persimmon, serviceberry, eastern redbud, flowering dogwood, black tupelo, American holly, red and sugar maples, white ash, blackberry, early saxifrage, hepatica, spring beauty, Dutchman's-breeches, trout lily, white trillium, bird's-foot and lance-leaved violets, phlox, columbine, dwarf iris, bladderwort, blue chicory, butterfly weed, fire pink, arrowroot, and jack-in-the-pulpit.

NEARBY POINTS OF INTEREST

The area surrounding the park offers other fascinating natural and cultural attractions that can be enjoyed as day trips or overnight excursions. Nolin Lake, which is a reservoir, is located ten miles north. Daniel Boone National Forest is about 125 miles to the east, and Cumberland Gap National Historical Park in Middlesboro is about 190 miles to the east. Abraham Lincoln Birthplace National Historic Site is about 35 miles northeast in Hodgenville. Part of Big South Fork National River and Recreation Area is also located in southeastern Kentucky.

REV. MARTIN LUTHER KING, JR.

1929 — 1968

"Free at last, Free at last,
Thank God Almighty

MARTIN LUTHER KING, JR., NATIONAL HISTORIC SITE

▲ Gravesite

Martin Luther King, Jr., National Historic Site

450 Auburn Avenue, N.E.
Atlanta, GA 30312-0522
404-331-5190

Established in 1980, this 36-acre national historic site protects and interprets the birthplace, church, and grave of Dr. Martin Luther King, Jr. (1929-1968), the African-American civil rights leader, minister, and author who was killed by an assassin's bullet on April 4, 1968. The site also includes the Martin Luther King, Jr., Center for Nonviolent Social Change, which was founded in 1968 to continue striving for social and economic equality. Adjacent to the site is a three-unit, 68-acre historic preservation district with a number of other buildings. Much of Atlanta's close-knit African-American community lived in this district, known as "Sweet Auburn," which prospered during the early 20th century.

King, the recipient of the 1964 Nobel Peace Prize, is perhaps best remembered for his eloquent "I Have a Dream" speech, delivered from the steps of the Lincoln Memorial during the March on Washington in 1963. That speech included this beloved passage: "I have a dream that one day on the red hills of Georgia, sons of former slaves and sons of former slave owners will be able to sit down together at a table of brotherhood. . . . I have a dream that my four little children will one day live in a nation where they will not be judged by the color of their skin, but by the content of their character. This is our hope. This is the faith that I go back to the South with. With this faith we will be able to hew out of the mountain of despair a stone of hope."

1895, then bought by King's grandfather, and occupied by the Williams-King family for 32 years; King was born there on January 15, 1929; **Ebenezer Baptist Church**, at 407-13 Auburn Avenue—a Gothic Revival structure completed in 1922, where King, his father, and grandfather were ministers; as the center of the community, the church's role went beyond religious matters to support "the advancement of black people and every righteous and social movement"; **The Martin Luther King, Jr., Center for Nonviolent Social Change**, at 449 Auburn Avenue—the organization founded in 1968 and headed by King's widow, Coretta Scott King, which continues to work toward King's dream of economic and social equality; **Big Bethel African Methodist Episcopal Church**, at 220 Auburn Avenue—a church built in the 1890s and rebuilt in 1924; its most prominent feature, the "Jesus Saves" sign on the steeple, was added when the structure was rebuilt after a 1920 fire; **Wheat Street Baptist Church**, at 365 Auburn Avenue—a church built between 1920 and 1931 that has been a community institution since its founding; **Odd Fellows Building and Auditorium**, at 228-50 Auburn Avenue—a six-story complex built between 1912 and 1914 to provide Sweet Auburn residents with space for offices, stores, and meetings; **Prince Hall Masonic Building**, at 332-34 Auburn Avenue—a building constructed in 1941 by Georgia's most influential black Masonic lodge and which currently houses the national offices of the Southern Christian Leadership Conference; **Royal Peacock Club**, at 184-86 Auburn Avenue—an entertainment spot known as the Top Hat until 1948, which has boasted such performers as Cab Calloway, Louis Armstrong, and Aretha Franklin; and **Atlanta Municipal Market**, at 209 Edgewood Avenue—a market still in operation where, even during the years of legal segregation in Atlanta, both blacks and whites shopped for fresh produce and meats.

OUTSTANDING FEATURES

The outstanding features of this site include the following historic structures: **Martin Luther King, Jr., Birth Home**, at 501 Auburn Avenue—a Queen Anne-style home built in

PRACTICAL INFORMATION

When to Go

The site is open daily.

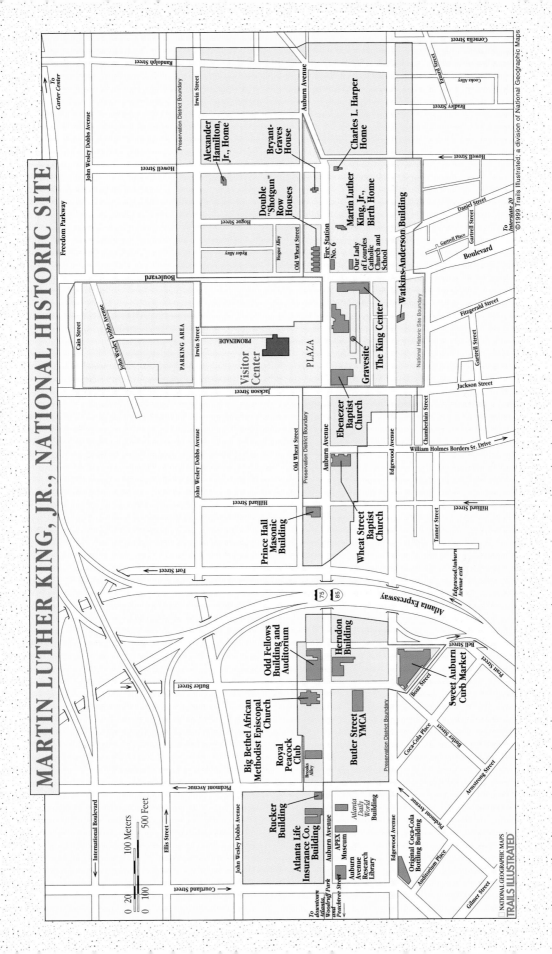

MARTIN LUTHER KING, JR., NATIONAL HISTORIC SITE

©1999 Trails Illustrated, a division of National Geographic Maps

NATIONAL GEOGRAPHIC MAPS
TRAILS ILLUSTRATED

How to Get There

By Car: Take I-75/85 northbound to the Edgewood/Auburn Avenue exit and follow signs to the site. Or take I-75/85 southbound to the Butler Street exit and follow signs to the site. Parking is available only in the lot on Edgewood Avenue, which is next to the Watkins-Anderson Building at 443-45 Edgewood Avenue.

By Air: Hartsfield International Airport (404-530-6830) is served by most major airlines.

By Train: Amtrak (800-872-7245) has a stop in Brookwood Station.

By Bus: Greyhound Lines (800-231-2222) has stops in Atlanta.

Fees and Permits

There are no entrance fees.

Visitor Center

Open daily. Information, interpretive exhibits, an interpretive film, publications, and schedule of activities. A gift shop is located in the King Center.

Facilities

There are limited facilities at the site.

Handicapped Accessibility

The King Center, Ebenezer Baptist Church, and the first floor of the birth home are wheelchair-accessible. A photo album shows the second floor of the birth home, and an interpretive film is captioned for the hearing-impaired. Cassette and braille versions of the official park brochure are available at the visitor center.

Medical Services

A hospital on Boulevard Avenue is one-half mile from the site.

Pets

Pets are not permitted in any public building.

ACTIVITIES

Options include ranger-guided tours of Martin Luther King, Jr.'s, birth home and additional activities at key sites provided seasonally by the National Park Service and private organizations. A visitor center provides interpretive exhibits, an auditorium for audiovisual programs, other basic visitor facilities, and publications.

OVERNIGHT STAYS

Lodging and Dining

Numerous lodging and dining facilities are located in Atlanta.

NEARBY POINTS OF INTEREST

The area surrounding this site offers other fascinating attractions that can be enjoyed as day trips or overnight excursions. The Chattahoochee River National Recreation Area is just north of downtown Atlanta; Kennesaw Mountain National Battlefield Park is northwest of Atlanta; and Ocmulgee National Monument and Oconee and Chattahoochee national forests are to the south.

VIRGIN ISLANDS NATIONAL PARK

▲ Annaberg Sugar Mill ruins

VIRGIN ISLANDS NATIONAL PARK

6310 Estate Nazareth
Charlotte Amalie, St. Thomas, VI
00802-1102
340-776-6201

This 14,688-acre national park on the subtropical West Indian island of St. John in the U.S. Virgin Islands, protects beautiful white coral-sand beaches; peaceful coves and bays; ecologically rich fringing and patch reefs of coral beneath blue-green waters; lushly vegetated hills; and the remnants of Danish colonial sugar plantations. Today, more than half of this small rugged island of volcanic origin is protected, thanks to the foresight and generosity of philanthropist Laurance S. Rockefeller and the Jackson Hole Preserve Corporation. The park was established in 1956 and was designated a Biosphere Reserve in 1976.

OUTSTANDING FEATURES

Among the many outstanding features of the park are the following: **Trunk Bay**, one of the most beautiful beaches in the world, with a self-guiding snorkel trail; **Hawksnest Bay**, an excellent quiet place for beginning snorkelers to view a reef in shallow water; **Leinster Bay**, one of the best snorkeling areas in the park, notably around Waterlemon Cay; **Cinnamon Bay**, an area with the park's campground that offers a good place for park visitors to base; and **Annaberg Sugar Mill**, ruins of an 18th-century mill that for two centuries produced raw sugar, molasses, and rum.

64

PRACTICAL INFORMATION

When to Go

The park is open year-round. The peak visitor season is from mid-December through mid-

April. Year-round temperatures vary little from the average of 79 degrees. The weather is usually delightful.

How to Get There

The main entrance is located near Cruz Bay at the ferry dock and visitor center.

By Air: The Harry S Truman Airport on the island of St. Thomas and the Alexander Hamilton Airport on the island of St. Croix are served by major carriers from the U.S. mainland and from San Juan, Puerto Rico. Seaplanes fly directly to Cruz Bay from Charlotte Amalie, Christiansted, St. Croix, and San Juan.

By Boat: Two passenger ferries run between St. Thomas and Cruz Bay: Red Hook Ferry (hourly 7 a.m. to 11 p.m.) and Charlotte Amalie Ferry (various schedules). Water taxi service is also available. Ferry service is provided from the nearby island of Tortola in the British Virgin Islands.

Fees and Permits

A fee of $4 is charged for visiting Trunk Bay and $4 for visiting the Annaberg Sugar Mill ruins.

Visitor Center

Cruz Bay Visitor Center and Biosphere Reserve Center: open daily. Interpretive exhibits, an audiovisual program, and publications. For more information, call 340-776-6201.

Facilities

Available are picnic areas, a campground in the park and another nearby, cold showers, and a water sports center, with sailing, scuba, and snorkeling tours, and with scuba, snorkeling, and sailboarding gear rentals. Cruz Bay has grocery stores, restaurants, a post office, a bank, laundry facilities, service station, Immigration and Customs police, and a first-aid clinic.

Handicapped Accessibility

Some beaches, the visitor center, and some campsites at Cinnamon Bay Campground are

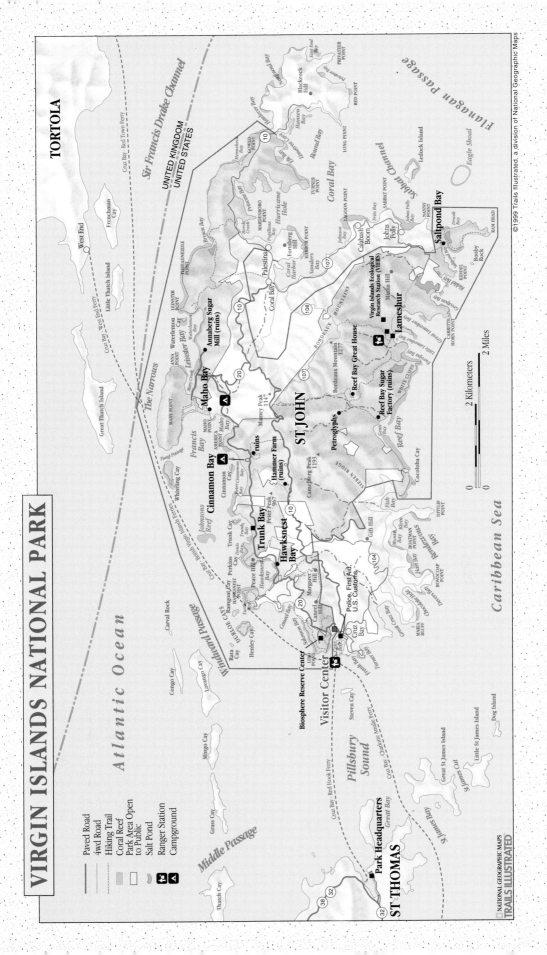

VIRGIN ISLANDS NATIONAL PARK

TORTOLA

Sir Francis Drake Channel

UNITED KINGDOM
UNITED STATES

Flanagan Passage

©1999 Trails Illustrated, a division of National Geographic Maps

Paved Road
4wd Road
Hiking Trail
Coral Reef
Park Area Open
to Public
Salt Pond
Ranger Station
Campground

Atlantic Ocean

The Narrows

Windward Passage

Middle Passage

Pillsbury Sound

Caribbean Sea

ST JOHN

ST THOMAS

Coral Bay

Francis Bay

Leinster Bay

Maho Bay

Cinnamon Bay

Trunk Bay

Hawksnest Bay

Annaberg Sugar Mill (ruins)

Hammer Farm (ruins)

Reef Bay Great House

Reef Bay Sugar Factory (ruins)

Petroglyphs

Virgin Islands Ecological
Research Station (VIERS)

Lameshur

Saltpond Bay

Reef Bay

BORDEAUX MOUNTAINS

Bordeaux Mountain 1277

Camelberg Peak 1193

Mamey Peak 967

SIEBEN RIDGE

Coral Bay

Palestina

Cruz Bay

Visitor Center

Police, First Aid
U.S. Customs

Biosphere Reserve Center

Park Headquarters
Great Bay

2 Kilometers
2 Miles

NATIONAL GEOGRAPHIC MAPS
TRAILS ILLUSTRATED

wheelchair-accessible. Annaberg Sugar Mill and ferries are accessible with assistance.

Medical Services

First aid is available in the park, and medical services are available throughout the island. A clinic is located in Cruz Bay.

Pets

Pets must be leashed at all times. They are not permitted on beaches, in the campground, or in picnic areas.

Safety and Regulations

For your safety and enjoyment and for the protection of the park, please follow these regulations and suggestions:

- Drive on the left side of the road. Sound your horn at blind curves.

- Use insect repellent to guard against mosquitoes and sand flies.

- Protect yourself from overexposure by using sunscreen and wearing hats and T-shirts.

- Because some plants are poisonous, notably the manchineel, do not touch or taste any unfamiliar plants.

- Hikers are advised to wear loose clothing.

- Protect yourself against sunburn, insects, and thorny vegetation and hike in appropriately sturdy shoes (not sandals).

- Swimmers are urged to use extreme caution when entering or leaving the ocean when the surf is high. Do not bodysurf and never swim alone. Do not stand on reefs or touch or scrape coral and other marine life. Scuba diving is not permitted off designated swimming beaches.

- Water-skiing and the use of personal watercraft (e.g., Jet Skis/Wave Runners) are prohibited in park waters.

- Beach fires are not permitted.

- Defacing, breaking, or removing natural or historical features on the island or in the water is prohibited.

- Anchor boats in sand well away from coral

reefs and sea grass beds or use mooring buoys where provided. Anchoring is prohibited in Salt Pond, Great Lameshur, and Reef Bays; moorings must be used in these areas. Staying aboard a boat in park waters is limited to 14 days in any 12-month period.

- Park waters are open to fishing with handheld rods. Fishing is not allowed in all of Trunk Bay or in buoy-designated swimming areas. Possession of spearguns within the park is strictly prohibited.

ACTIVITIES

Options include swimming, snorkeling, snorkel tours, scuba diving, boating, boat cruises, sailing, hiking, birdwatching, picnicking, camping, fishing, interpretive walks and talks, and history tours. Further information is available in the park's newspaper, *Kapok Chronicle*.

Hiking Trails

Trails for hiking include the following:

North Shore Trails: **Lind Point Trail**, a 1.1-mile route beginning at the visitor center, leading through an arid, cactus-and-dry-scrub, open forest habitat, climbing to Lind Point Overlook at 160 feet elevation, and ending at Caneel Bay's Honeymoon Beach; **Caneel Hill Trail**, a 2.4-mile route beginning at the village of Cruz Bay; at .8-of-a-mile, trail reaches the summit of Caneel Hill at 719 feet elevation, climbs 848-foot Margaret Hill, and steeply descends through forest to Northshore Road; **Cinnamon Bay Self-Guided Trail**, a half-mile interpretive loop beginning and ending a few yards to the east of the Cinnamon Bay Campground entrance road, leading through a shady area of native trees, and affording an opportunity to view the site of an old sugar factory; **Cinnamon Bay Trail**, a 1.1-mile route beginning 100 yards east of the Cinnamon Bay Campground entrance road and following an old Danish plantation road through a forested stretch and up to Centerline Road; **Francis Bay Trail**, a half-mile route beginning at the western end of the paved Mary Creek Road, leading through dry-scrub forest habitat, passing the historic Francis Bay Estate House, and ending at the beach; swimming and snorkeling are popular here, but visitors are cautioned to be especially careful as there are no lifeguards on this beach; a brackish pond and mangroves offer good opportunities for birdwatching; **Annaberg Sugar Mill Ruins Trail**, a short, self-guided interpretive route beginning at Annaberg picnic site, leading up to this historic refinery above Leinster Bay, and providing a beautiful view across Sir Francis Drake Channel to the British West Indies island of Tortola; and **Leinster Bay Trail/Road**, an .8-mile route beginning at Annaberg picnic site and following eastward the unpaved Leinster Bay Road to Waterlemon Bay; swimming in the bay and snorkeling around Waterlemon Cay are excellent, but visitors are cautioned to be especially careful as there are no lifeguards on this beach.

South Shore Trails: **Reef Bay Trail**, a 2.2-mile route beginning 4.9 miles to the east of Cruz Bay village on Centerline Road; descending through damp, shady forest with a great diversity of plantlife; passing the ruins of four sugar estates; and reaching the island's south shore at Reef Bay, near which are a picnic site and the ruins of Reef Bay Sugar Mill; no lifeguards are stationed on this beach; the National Park Service offers scheduled interpreter-led hikes on the trail, with the return by boat to Cruz Bay; **Bordeaux Mountain Trail**, a 1.2-mile trail beginning on Bordeaux Mountain Road at 1.7 miles southwest of its junction with Centerline Road, descending steeply 1,000 feet on an unshaded route, and reaching the shore of Little Lameshur Bay where there is a picnic area and the end of Little Lameshur Bay Road; **Yawzi Point Trail**, a one-third-mile route beginning near the end of Little Lameshur Bay Road, and leading to the end of this narrow, thorn-scrub-covered point, along the shore of which are a number of small coves; **Salt Pond Bay Trail**, a .2-mile trail beginning at a parking area 3.9 miles south of Coral Bay on the road between Coral Bay and Lameshur and leading through cactus-scrub habitat and down to Salt Pond Bay beach, where there is a picnic area; while swimming and snorkeling are good here, visitors are cautioned that this area is usually

hot and sunny and that there are no lifeguards stationed on this beach; and **Ram Head Trail**, a one-mile, exposed, normally sunny and hot route beginning at the southern end of Salt Pond Bay beach, leading through cactus-scrub habitat to a blue-cobble beach, and switchbacking to the 200-foot-high crest of windswept Ram Head; hikers are cautioned to be careful along the edge of the cliffs at this southernmost point on St. John.

OVERNIGHT STAYS

Lodging and Dining

While there are no lodging facilities within the park, St. John offers a wide range of accommodations, including guest houses, homes for rent, and beach resorts. Meals are served at Cruz Bay, Trunk Bay, and Cinnamon Bay. St. Thomas also offers many lodging and dining facilities. Contact a travel agent for further information.

Camping

Cinnamon Bay Campground, with tent sites and two group sites, is open all year. Three types of camping opportunities are available: bare tent sites where campers provide their own tents and all their own camping gear; sites where canvas tents for four to six persons are provided; and one-room screened-in cottages that sleep four to six persons. Provisions at the latter two sites include cots, bedding linen, cooking and eating utensils, a charcoal grill, gas stove, and an ice chest. Reservations are required for all camping and can be made up to eight months in advance by contacting Cinnamon Bay Campground, P.O. Box 720, St. John, VI 00831; 800-539-9998 or 340-776-6226. Sites are usually booked up well in advance for the December 15 to April 15 peak camping period. The limit of stay for that period is 14 days; otherwise, it is 21 days. Group camping is available year-round with reservations. There are two group sites with eight canvas tents for four to six people each. Cots, linens, cooking and eating utensils, a charcoal grill, a gas stove, and an ice chest are provided.

FLORA AND FAUNA (Partial Listings)

Mammals: fish-eating, cave, mastiff, fruit-eating, and red fig-eating bats, and the exotic Indian mongoose.

Birds: white-tailed tropicbird, brown booby, brown pelican, magnificent frigatebird, little blue and green-backed herons, yellow-crowned night heron, cattle egret, white-cheeked pintail (Bahama duck), American wigeon, red-tailed hawk, American kestrel, clapper rail, common moorhen, Wilson's and black-bellied plovers, greater and lesser yellowlegs, solitary and spotted sandpipers, American oystercatcher, black-necked stilt, laughing gull, royal tern, scaly-naped pigeon, Zenaida and common ground doves, bridled quail-dove, mangrove cuckoo, smooth-billed ani, green-throated carib and Antillean crested hummingbird, belted kingfisher, Puerto Rican flycatcher, gray kingbird, Caribbean elaenia, mockingbird, pearly-eyed thrasher, black-whiskered vireo, yellow warbler (numerous other warblers during spring and autumn migrations), bananaquit, black-faced grassquit, lesser Antillean bullfinch, and shiny cowbird.

Fishes and other marine life: corals (elkhorn, staghorn, fire, star, tube, pillar, and brain), seafan, seawhip, seaplume, sponges, sea urchins, sea anemone, sea cucumbers, starfishes, brittlestars, spiny lobster, shrimp, crabs, moray eel, angelfish, parrotfish, yellowtail, grouper, blue tang, trumpetfish, trunkfish, triggerfish, surgeonfish, snapper, bonito, spotted goatfish, sergeant major, beau gregory, jewel fish, butterfly fish, yellow grunt, porkfish, spiny squirrelfish, blue-headed wrasse, cowfish, octopus, sting ray, barracuda, nurse shark, and sea turtles.

Trees, Shrubs, and Flowers: (*non-native species)

Tropical moist forest species: teyer (tyre) palm, bay rum tree, kapok, hog-plum, wild-mammey, monkey-pistol, trumpet tree, soursop, and mango*.

Tropical dry forest species: Ginger Thomas tree, gumbo limbo (turpentine tree), wild frangipani, catch-and-keep (acacia), native calabash, poison-ash (leaves resemble holly), black and white mampoo trees, wild tamarind*, and lime*.

Species generally in both moist and dry forest: wattapama, starvation tree (pain-killer tree), pinguin (wild pinneaple), and South American genip*.

Shore species: seagrape; manchineel (extremely poisonous); red, white, and black mangroves; and coconut palm*.

Other plantlife includes: century plant (*Agave missionum*); bromeliad (air plant); beach morning-glory; Christmas orchid; and a number of cacti, including dildo (organ pipe), Turk's-cap, night-blooming cereus, and woolly nipple.

NEARBY POINTS OF INTEREST

The area surrounding the park offers other fascinating natural and cultural attractions that can be enjoyed as day trips or overnight excursions. Christiansted National Historic Site, Buck Island Reef National Monument, and Salt River Bay National Historical Park and Ecological Preserve are all on the nearby island of St. Croix.

OTHER NATIONAL PARK UNITS IN THE SOUTHEAST REGION

▲ *Sunrise, Biscayne National Park, Florida*

Other National Park Units in the Southeast Region

ALABAMA

Horseshoe Bend National Military Park

Route 1, Box 103
Daviston, AL 36256-9751
205-234-7111

This 2,040-acre national military park along Horseshoe Bend of the Tallapoosa River in eastern Alabama protects and interprets the site of a battle on March 27, 1814, in which more than 3,500 U.S. infantrymen, Tennessee militiamen, and Indian allies under the command of Major Gen. Andrew Jackson defeated 1,000 Red Stick warriors of the Upper Creek Indians. At least 800 Indian warriors were killed and 350 women and children were taken captive, while only 49 of Jackson's soldiers were killed. The battle ended the Creek Indian War and added three-fifths of present-day Alabama and one-fifth of Georgia to the United States.

The visitor center provides interpretive exhibits, an audiovisual program, and publications; two picnic areas are also available. A three-mile drive loops through Horseshoe Bend and the site of the Upper Creeks' Tohopeka Village; a 2.8-mile, self-guided interpretive trail descends from the overlook on Cotton Patch Hill through the battlefield and along the riverbank. Visitors are urged to be alert for poisonous snakes, fire ants, and poison ivy. The park occasionally presents living-history demonstrations, the most important of which is held during the last weekend of March. Two picnic areas are available. While camping is not permitted, a campground is available in nearby Wind Creek State Park. The park is open daily, except Thanksgiving, Christmas, and New Year's Day. Access from Birmingham is southeast about 90 miles on U.S. Route 280 and north 12 miles on State Route 49.

Little River Canyon National Preserve

P.O. Box 45
Fort Payne, AL 35967-3673
205-997-9239

This national preserve on the Cumberland Plateau of northeast Alabama comprises 35 miles of the Little River—one of the most spectacular canyons in the eastern United States. Often called the "Grand Canyon of the East," the preserve offers world-class whitewater float and kayaking trips. Erosion has created a variety of scenic rock expanses, benches, and bluffs. Although NPCA has long advocated protection of the canyon as a unit of the National Park System, at this time the National Park Service has not yet acquired the land from private owners, and no public facilities are available.

Russell Cave National Monument

3729 County Road 98
Bridgeport, AL 35740-9770
205-495-2672

This 310-acre national monument in Alabama's northeast corner protects a limestone cave in which the evidence of almost continuous human occupation dates back some 8,000 years. Archaeological research carried out since 1953 by the National Geographic Society, the Smithsonian Institution, and the National Park Service has revealed the cultural periods in which the cave was frequently inhabited, probably as a winter home. These periods include the Earliest Archaic Period from roughly 7000 to 5500 B.C., Early Archaic from around 5500 to 4500 B.C., Middle Archaic from around 4500 to 3500 B.C., Late Archaic from roughly 3500 to 500 B.C., the Woodland Period from 500 B.C. to A.D. 1000, and the Mississippian Period from A.D. 1000 to 1500. The earlier inhabitants of this area gathered nuts, seeds, and berries and hunted wild animals, while later Indians relied increasingly upon agriculture, settled in villages, made pottery, and produced ornaments of bone and shell. Cultural changes like these have been traced through such clues as the shape and size of projectile points, tools, and utensils.

Interpretive exhibits, an audiovisual program, guided tours of the cave, and demonstrations of ancient Indian life are provided. The monument is open year-round, except on Thanksgiving, Christmas, and New Year's Day. Access to Russell Cave is eight miles from U.S. Route 72 at Bridgeport, north on County Road 75 to Mount Carmel, and east on County Road 98 to the entrance.

Selma to Montgomery National Historic Trail

**National Park Service
1924 Building
100 Alabama Street, SW
Atlanta, GA 30303
404-562-3175**

This 54-mile trail extends along U.S. Route 80 from Selma to the Alabama state capital in Montgomery. The trail commemorates a three-day march in 1965, which was organized by Dr. Martin Luther King, Jr., and the Southern Christian Leadership Conference. The demonstration helped focus national attention on the need for the Voting Rights Act. Just 134 days after the march, Congress passed the legislation, which was signed into law on August 6, 1965, by President Lyndon B. Johnson.

Tuskegee Airmen National Historic Site

**c/o National Park Service
Southeast Regional Office
Atlanta Federal Center-1924 Building,
100 Alabama St., S.W.
Atlanta, GA 30303
404-562-3182**

Prior to World War II, African Americans were not allowed to train at U.S. military facilities. What began as an experiment at Tuskegee Institute's Moton Field in Alabama resulted in the nation's first aviation training school for African Americans. The National Park Service now honors the memory of these pioneering and courageous fighter pilots of the 99th Squadron, who flew and fought over the skies of Italy and the Mediterranean during the war, by including the field and its remaining structures in the park system as the Tuskegee Airmen National Historic Site. This is the first park unit with a primary purpose of interpreting the struggle of African Americans to integrate the U.S. Armed Forces.

Tuskegee Institute National Historic Site

**P.O. Drawer 10
Tuskegee, AL 36088
205-727-6390**

This 57-acre national historic site in eastern Alabama celebrates the founding of the Tuskegee Institute by Booker T. Washington in 1881. When Washington, who was born a slave, founded what was originally called the Tuskegee Normal and Industrial Institute, there were 30 African-American students who attended classes in a run-down church and shanty. In the post-Reconstruction era, marked by growing segregation and disenfranchisement of black citizens, the institute provided training for teachers and taught occupational skills to equip students for work in agriculture and the trades. Many of the institute's buildings were erected during Washington's lifetime; they were designed by R. R. Taylor, the first African American to graduate from the Massachusetts Institute of Technology, and were built by the students themselves. Today, Tuskegee has more than 160 buildings and 5,000 students.

Visitors may tour the campus on foot or by car. The visitor orientation center, open daily except on Thanksgiving, Christmas, and New Year's Day, is located in the Carver Museum, where audiovisual programs are presented. Guided tours are offered at The Oaks, Washington's former home. To reach the site, exit I-85 south onto State Route 81, turn west (right) onto Old Montgomery Road, and follow signs to the visitor orientation center.

ARKANSAS

Arkansas Post National Memorial

**1741 Old Post Road
Gillett, AR 72055
870-548-2207**

This 389-acre national memorial on the banks of the Arkansas River in southeast Arkansas honors all those of many cultures and nationalities who, with courage and sacrifice, endured hardships and risked or lost their lives in the settlement and early development of frontier lands that became part of the United States. More specifically, it commemorates nearly three centuries of events related to the successive ownership of the vast surrounding region, of which Arkansas is a small part. This region was initially claimed by France, beginning in the 1680s; then by Spain from 1762 to 1800; briefly again by France; and, after the landmark Louisiana Purchase in 1804, finally owned by the United States. Early events included the construction of French and Spanish trading posts, settlements, and forts, as well as numerous encounters between Native American and European cultures. In 1783, British soldiers and their sympathizers launched a brief, unsuccessful, post-Revolutionary War attack against the garrison of a Spanish fort in retaliation for Spain's support of American independence. Subsequently, Americans established a frontier fur-trading settlement, a territorial capital, and a thriving river port. And in 1863, a Civil War battle occurred here, in which a 30,000-man Union force with a fleet of gunboats sailed up-river and unleashed a heavy bombardment, defeating the 5,000-man garrison at a Confederate fortification.

The memorial's visitor center provides interpretive exhibits, an audiovisual film, and publications. Self-guided interpretive trails lead visitors to some of the historic sites and through some of the natural habitats. The National Park Service urges hikers to be alert for poisonous snakes, ticks, chiggers, and poison ivy. A picnic area is available. Access to the memorial from Little Rock is southeast 84 miles on U.S. Route 65 to Dumas, then north 15 miles on U.S. Route 165, and east two miles on State Route 169.

Buffalo National River

P.O. Box 1173
Harrison, AR 72601
870-741-5443

This 94,309-acre national river in the Ozark Mountains of northern Arkansas protects 137 miles of the Buffalo River—one of the few remaining unpolluted free-flowing rivers in the lower 48 states. Among the area's attractions are colorful cliffs rising to 500 feet above the river, weather-sculpted rock formations, caves, waterfalls, springs, lush forests, and numerous pre-Columbian and historic sites ranging from bluff shelters once occupied by archaic Indians to cabins built by early settlers. The river is popular for float trips by canoe or kayak; trips range from half-day to ten-day excursions. Canoe-launching sites, canoe rentals, and guided canoe trips are all available. The National Park Service warns visitors to stay away from the river during periods of high water. Other activities include hiking, bird-watching, swimming, fishing, picnicking, camping, and public hunting on undeveloped parts of the river during the designated season.

The Tyler Bend Visitor Center, near where U.S. Route 65 crosses the river, is open daily, except Thanksgiving, Christmas, and New Year's Day, and provides interpretive exhibits, information on float trips, and publications. Information centers are located at Buffalo Point, near where State Route 14 crosses the river, and at Pruitt, where State Route 7 crosses the river. Interpretive programs and walks are offered, and hiking trails range from short routes at Buffalo Point, Pruitt, and Lost Valley to longer ones leading into Ponca and Lower Buffalo wilderness areas. Visitors are cautioned to be alert for poisonous snakes and ticks. Fourteen campgrounds are open year-round on a first-come, first-served basis. Fees are charged at Buffalo Point Campground from April through October. Buffalo Point has a restaurant (open seasonally) and concession-operated cabins (for reservations, contact Buffalo Point Concessions, HCR #66, Box 388, Yellville, AR 72687; 501-449-6206). Services at the national river are reduced during the winter. Access to the main area of visitor activities at Buffalo Point is 14 miles south of Yellville on State Route 14 and east three miles on State Route 268. The visitor center is 32 miles south of Harrison on U.S. Route 65.

Fort Smith National Historic Site

P.O. Box 1406
Fort Smith, AR 72902-1406
501-783-3961

This 75-acre national historic site at the junction of the Arkansas and Poteau rivers in western Arkansas protects and interprets the remains of two 19th-century forts and a historic federal court house. The first fortification was a small log-and-stone stockade where U.S. troops were stationed to promote peaceful relations between the native Osage Indians and the Cherokee emigrants as the Cherokee were forced by white leaders to leave their traditional homelands to the east. In 1822, when successful negotiations resolved most divisive issues between the two tribes and resulted in a promise that white men would not settle on Indian lands, Fort Smith was abandoned.

But then, beginning in 1829, the U.S. government implemented an increasingly aggressive policy of forcing Indian tribes out of the southeastern states and relocating them by the thousands in a brutal campaign of ethnic cleansing. As white settlers became fearful of the influx of Indian refugees in and around Arkansas, the U.S. Army began constructing a second fort in 1838. However, as it became clear that the Indians would remain peaceful, the fort was converted to a supply center. During the Civil War, the fort was initially occupied by Confederate troops and then by Union soldiers. In 1865, a Grand Council of Indians held at Fort Smith prepared for the signing of treaties that took away from the tribes about half the lands previously declared as their reservation. From 1875 to 1896, the Federal Court for the Western District of Arkansas occupied the fort.

The visitor center, located in the barracks-courthouse-jail building that dates from 1849, provides interpretive exhibits, an audiovisual program, and publications. The site is open daily, except Thanksgiving, Christmas, and New Year's Day. Access from U.S. Route 64 (Garrison Avenue) is south two blocks on 4th Street and west (right) onto Parker Avenue to the entrance.

Little Rock Central High School National Historic Site

c/o National Park Service
Midwest Office
1709 Jackson St.
Omaha, NE 68102-2571
402-221-3448

The 1954 Supreme Court decision in *Brown v. Board of Education* spurred the admission of nine African American students to Central High School in Little Rock, Arkansa in 1957. Their attendance at Central High began the slow process of desegregation in public schools throughout the nation, particularly in the South. Compelled by the magnitude of white mob violence, President Eisenhower issued federal troops to usher the childeren into the school safely—the first use of federal force to support African-American civil rights. In 1998, the high school became a national historic site and one of the newest units of the park system to recognize and interpret the significant role the school played in the Civil Rights Movement. Little Rock Central High School appears much as it did more than 40 years ago and still serves its original purpose as a large urban high school.

Pea Ridge National Military Park

P.O. Box 700
Pea Ridge, AR 72751-0700
501-451-8122

This 4,300-acre national military park in northwest Arkansas protects and interprets the site of a Civil War battle of March 7-8, 1862. In one of the war's major engagements west of the Mississippi River, Union troops overwhelmed the exhausted Confederate forces and about 1,000 Cherokee. The heaviest fighting occurred near a hostelry called Elkhorn Tavern and along the Union supply line on Telegraph Road. The defeat of the Confederates ended their plan to invade Missouri, a key border state that remained in the Union.

The visitor center provides interpretive exhibits, slide programs, and publications. A seven-mile, self-guided interpretive tour leads visitors to a number of key points of interest, and Elkhorn Tavern is open for tours from Memorial Day through October as staffing allows. Ten miles of hiking trails and an 11-mile equestrian trail also wind through the area. The park is open daily, except Thanksgiving, Christmas, and New Year's Day. Access is north ten miles from Rogers on U.S. Route 62.

Biscayne National Park

P.O. Box 1369
Homestead, FL 33090-1369
305-230-7275

This 172,924-acre national park along the southeast coast of Florida protects an ecologically rich area, only 5 percent of which consists of land. The marine gardens include the northernmost coral reef in the United States, a strip of mangrove-fringed mainland shore, and a narrow chain of more than 40 subtropical barrier islands (the northern extension of the Florida Keys), bounded by Biscayne Bay and the Atlantic Ocean. With the park's waters teeming with marine life, popular ways to enjoy the park include scuba diving, snorkeling, canoeing, kayaking, sailing, and interpretive reef cruises. Tropical hardwood hammocks and bordering mangroves also provide rich island habitats for an abundance of wildlife, including wading and other birds. The area was established as a national monument in 1968; in 1980, it was expanded and redesignated a national park.

Among the park's 250 species of fish are angelfish, parrot fish, porkfish, blue tang, squirrelfish, blue-striped grunt, snapper, grouper, yellowtails, wrasses, gobies, filefish, barracuda, cowfish, goatfish, trunkfish, Spanish hogfish, stingray, moray eel, and bull shark. Other marine life includes many species of coral, sea fans (a form of soft coral), sea whips, sponges, starfish, spiny lobster, crabs, shrimp, plume worms, sea anemones, squid, stingray, and sea turtles. Alligators and crocodiles inhabit the park's waters—the former preferring fresh water habitat and the latter favoring salt and brackish waters. Marine mammals are the slow-moving manatee and the bottlenose dolphin. Terrestrial mammals include raccoon and marsh rabbit. Just a few of the park's 170 bird species are frigate bird, anhinga, double-crested cormorant, white ibis, snowy egret, little blue heron, roseate spoonbill, wood stork, brown pelican, yellow-crowned night heron, laughing gull, royal tern, willet, reddish egret, swallow-tailed kite, short-tailed hawk, osprey, bald eagle, and white-crowned pigeon. Among the trees are red, black, and white mangroves, gumbo-limbo, buttonwood, West Indies mahogany, strangler fig, pigeon plum, wild lime, torchwood, Florida poison tree, seven-year apple, Jamaica dogwood, devil's-potato, satinleaf, joewood, geiger-tree, red-berried eugenia, and coconut and silver thatch (Sargent) palms.

Convoy Point Visitor Center, nine miles east of Homestead on North Canal Drive (SW 328 St.), provides interpretive exhibits, audio-visual programs (including a hurricane video), publications, and nautical charts. Canoe rentals are available adjacent to the visitor center. Reservations are required for snorkeling, diving, and glass-bottom boat tours that depart from Convoy Point; contact Biscayne National Underwater Park, P.O. Box 1270, Homestead, FL 33090; 305-230-1100. The park provides boat-in campgrounds with 14-day limits on a first-come, first-served basis on seven-mile-long Elliott Key (primitive tent sites designated) and Boca Chita Key (no sites designated). A ranger station is located on Elliott Key. Potable water is available only on Elliott Key. A picnic site is available on Adams Key. Boating restrictions are in effect to help protect the manatee, which is federally listed as endangered. Hiking trails, including a half-mile, self-guided nature trail through tropical hardwood hammock, are available on Elliott Key (free backcountry permits are required), and a half-mile nature trail leads visitors through a stretch of hardwood hammock on Adams Key. Mosquitoes and other insects can be annoying from April to December, so hikers and campers are advised to bring insect repellent. Further information is available in the newspaper, *Visitor's Guide to National Parks and Preserves of South Florida*.

Canaveral National Seashore

308 Julia Street
Titusville, FL 32796-3521
407-267-1110

This 57,661-acre national seashore, whose boundaries coincide with the Merritt Island National Wildlife Refuge, extends 24 miles along the east coast of central Florida. It protects an ecologically diverse, undeveloped barrier island containing beautiful Atlantic Ocean beaches, sand dunes, saltmarshes, mangrove swamps, tidal estuaries, freshwater ponds, pine woodlands, groves of cabbage palmetto, and hardwood hammocks. The latter are small, low-lying coastal islands with such evergreen hardwoods as ancient Spanish-moss-draped live oaks, torchwood, false-mastic, marbleberry, wild coffee, and white stopper eugenia. On the seaward side of dunes, a tall grass called sea oats helps to stabilize the sand against wind and water erosion; and seagrape, a shrubby tree with nearly circular, leathery leaves, is at the northern end of its range at Canaveral. On the inland side of dunes are dense thickets of low-growing saw palmetto, a species of yucca called Spanish bayonet, and a variety of prickly pear cactus.

The seashore's varied habitats support an abundance of wildlife. Terrestrial mammals include bobcat, raccoon, and armadillo. The alligator and an endangered marine mammal, the manatee, inhabit the waters of Indian River and Mosquito Lagoon. On summer nights, giant loggerhead and green sea turtles haul themselves onto the beaches to bury their eggs. Among more than 300 species of birds are herons, egrets, wood stork, white ibis, roseate spoonbill, many species of ducks (including the tens of thousands of waterfowl that winter in the area), shorebirds, bald eagle, osprey, scrub jay, and numerous songbirds, many of which migrate through the area.

An information center is located at the northern end of the seashore. Visitor activities include hiking, swimming, boating, sailing, canoeing, backcountry camping, and bird-watching. Public hunting is permitted in part of the seashore during the designated season. Among the hiking trails are the quarter-mile, self-guided interpretive Turtle Mound Trail that leads to the top of a pre-Columbian Timucuan Indian burial mound; a 12-mile stretch of ocean beach, beginning at the end of the road on Playalinda Beach; and two loop trails— Oak Hammock Trail in the seashore's south district and Eldora Hammock Trail in the north district—both of which offer opportunities for visitors to see the magical beauty of these lush, wooded hammocks. A self-guided canoe route also loops through the northern end of the seashore. The National Park Service urges swimmers to be aware of strong ocean currents and heavy surf and to be alert for stinging jellyfish, especially the Portuguese man-o'-war. Access to the seashore from New Smyrna Beach is seven miles south on State Route A1A to the north district; or from Titusville, 12 miles east on State Route 402 to the south district.

Castillo de San Marcos National Monument

1 Castillo Drive
St. Augustine, FL 32084-3699
904-829-6506

This 20-acre national monument in northeast Florida protects and interprets a massive Spanish colonial fort that was established in 1672 and was for many years the northern-most military outpost of Spain's widespread territorial claims in the Western Hemisphere. It is the oldest masonry (coquina stone) fort and the best-preserved example of Spanish colonial fortification in the continental United States. The fort has served many purposes over the years. It first successfully guarded from Spain's chief colonial rival, Britain, the hotly contested territory along what is today the coastline of Florida, Georgia, and the Carolinas. In 1702 and again in 1740, British forces launched attacks upon the fort but failed to break through its defenses. Then, at the end of the French and Indian War in 1763, Spain handed the fort over to Britain, and the British flag flew over the castillo for 21 years through America's War for Independence. Under the terms of the 1783 Treaty of Paris, Britain was forced to give Florida back to Spain, so the fort changed hands again, until finally in 1821 Florida was ceded to the United States and the fort was renamed Fort Marion. During the Seminole Indian War, the Civil War, and the Spanish-American War, the facility held prisoners of war.

Today, interpretive exhibits are installed in the fort's former storage rooms. Visitors may also enjoy interpretive programs, living-history demonstrations, and self-guided tours through the structure. The National Park Service urges visitors to be alert when walking through the fort, as there are uneven steps and rough surfaces. The monument is open daily, except Christmas. Access to the fort from I-95 is at State Route 16 exit and U.S. Route 1 to historic downtown St. Augustine.

De Soto National Memorial

P.O. Box 15390
Bradenton, FL 34280-5390
941-792-0458

This 26-acre national memorial at the mouth of the Manatee River in Tampa Bay on Florida's west coast commemorates the landing of Spanish explorer Hernando de Soto and his army near this site in 1539. De Soto and his successor, Luis de Moscoso, led a four-year, nearly 4,000-mile trek through the uncharted wilderness of what is today the southeastern United States. The Spanish Crown had given the explorer a license "to conquer, pacify, and populate" the region then called La Florida.

The roughly 700-member De Soto expedition consisted of a large force of soldiers; construction engineers and carpenters for building boats, bridges, and temporary encampment shelters; a number of Roman Catholic friars; and a few women. There were also more than 200 horses and other livestock. The Spaniards expected to discover gold and other sources of wealth, as had previously occurred in Peru and Mexico, but their reward instead was having to endure seemingly unending hardships and misery. The expedition repeatedly encountered Indians. While a few of these encounters were peaceful, others erupted in warfare, with Indian warriors retaliating against the ruthlessness and harsh demands of the Spaniards. Throughout the expedition, many Indians were taken as slaves, others were slaughtered, and women were taken captive. Some of those who resisted were burned at the stake, shot, or had a hand cut off as an example to the others. The largest of the confrontations occurred in Alabama, when the expedition found itself suddenly surrounded by several hundred Mabila warriors angered by De Soto's demand that the tribe provide several hundred of their people to serve as enslaved porters. A fierce battle raged, in which more than 2,000 Indians were killed, their village destroyed, and some of De Soto's most valued colleagues killed. Even more devastating to the native populations of the region than the battles and killing were the ravaging epidemics of such European-introduced diseases as typhoid, smallpox, and measles, against which the Indians had little or no natural immunity.

The memorial today contains a rich variety of flora and fauna. Mammals include red fox, armadillo, opossum, raccoon, and gray squirrel. Among the many bird species are the magnificent frigatebird, brown and white pelicans, green-backed and little blue herons, snowy and great egrets, wood stork, white ibis, roseate spoonbill, a number of gulls and terns, black skimmer, bald eagle, osprey, bobwhite, ground dove, pileated and red-bellied woodpeckers, blue jay, Carolina and house wrens, catbird, mockingbird, brown thrasher, yellow-throated and parula warblers, and cardinal. Trees include red, black, white, and button mangroves, along with the gumbo-limbo, southern red and bay cedars, cabbage palmetto, shrubby saw palmetto, the poisonous palm-like zamia, sea grape, strangler fig, live oak, groundsel tree, and southern bayberry (wax myrtle).

The visitor center provides interpretive exhibits, publications, and programs, including living-history demonstrations from late December to early April. A half-mile, self-guided nature trail leads visitors along the Manatee River shore of De Soto Point. A short spur trail leads to the ruins of an early 19th-century tabby house (tabby is a building material derived from ground-up oyster shells mixed with mud) from one of Florida's earliest-known American settlements. The National Park Service cautions hikers to be alert for poisonous snakes and poison ivy. Access to the memorial from I-75 is ten miles west on State Road 64 and 2.5 miles north on 75 Street NW (Manatee Avenue).

Dry Tortugas National Park

c/o Everglades National Park
40001 State Road 9336
Homestead, FL 33034-6733
305-242-7700

This 64,700-acre national park located nearly 70 miles west of Key West, Florida, protects a cluster of seven coral islands—the most pristine coral reef system in the continental United States. The islands were named the Dry Tortugas because of the lack of freshwater and for the loggerhead, hawksbill, and green sea turtles (tortugas in Spanish) that live and breed there. In addition to the magnificent fringing reef and patch reefs of more than 30 species of corals, there are areas of sea grass beds, sea whips, and sea fans. A tremendous variety of fishes inhabit the area, including angelfish, butterfly fish, grunts, jewfish, bigeye, tarpon, wahoos, groupers, amberjacks, snapper, barracuda, and sharks.

The bird population is also spectacular: nearly 300 species have been recorded, some breeding and others briefly passing through on migrations. Between March and September, approximately 100,000 sooty terns congregate on the Bush Key rookery for their breeding season. Other birds include the magnificent frigatebird, white-tailed tropicbird, brown and masked boobies, brown pelican, double-crested cormorant, great and snowy egrets, little blue and green-backed herons, osprey, black-bellied plover, ruddy turnstone, sanderling, laughing gull, royal tern, brown noddy, mourning dove, yellow-billed cuckoo, ruby-throated hummingbird, belted kingfisher, a number of swallows and thrushes, catbird, more than 20 species of warblers, scarlet and summer tanagers, rose-breasted grosbeak, indigo and painted buntings, savannah sparrow, bobolink, and Baltimore and orchard orioles.

The historical highlight of the park is Fort Jefferson, the largest brick and masonry structure in the Western Hemisphere and the largest of the forts from Maine to Texas. Construction on this fortification was begun in 1846, but was never completed and never saw military action. It served as a U.S. military prison during the Civil War. The fort was originally protected within Fort Jefferson National Monument in 1935. In the early 1980s, the National Parks and Conservation Association proposed renaming and redesignating the Dry Tortugas "to signify the importance of their marine resources and our national commitment to protect them." In 1992, the monument was redesignated as a national park.

The park provides docking and mooring facilities, a visitor center, picnic area, interpretive programs, and a self-guided tour of the fort. Visitor activities include swimming, snorkeling, diving, boating, sailing, fishing, and birdwatching. The National Park Service cautions swimmers to be alert for strong ocean currents and to avoid contact with sharp coral and the piercing spines of sea urchins.

Camping is permitted on Garden Key at a limited few sites. Access to the park is by boat or air taxi from Key West and elsewhere.

Florida National Scenic Trail

**U.S. Forest Service
227 N. Bronough Street, Suite 4061
Tallahassee, FL 32301
904 681-7293**

This national scenic trail extends 1,300 miles through Big Cypress National Preserve and several national and state forests and ends at Gulf Islands National Seashore near Pensacola. More than 600 miles are open to the public.

Fort Caroline National Memorial

**12713 Fort Caroline Road
Jacksonville, FL 32225-1240
904-641-7155**

This 138-acre national memorial protects and interprets the site of the initial attempt by France to start a new colonial empire in this region of North America. In 1564, 200 French Huguenots (Protestants) constructed a small, triangular-shaped fortification and settlement here, but after a few months of disillusioning hardships, 80 of the Frenchmen mutinied and sailed off to attack Spanish ships and settlements in the West Indies. In 1565, just as the remaining colonists were about to give up, a ship arrived with reinforcements. In the meantime, Spain, also trying to lay claim to the region, feared that the French settlement posed a threat to its shipping routes and other interests and also viewed the Huguenots as heretics and enemies of the Spanish Crown. Consequently, a month after the French reinforcements arrived, 500 Spaniards came ashore about 40 miles south of Fort Caroline, marched north, and launched an attack, capturing the settlement, and killing most of its inhabitants. Two years later, French soldiers in a surprise attack took back the fort, killing many of its Spanish defenders.

The visitor center, shared with Timucuan Ecological and Historic Preserve, provides interpretive exhibits, programs, and publications. A picnic area is available. Access to the memorial from downtown Jacksonville is east on State Route 10, north on either Monument Road or St. Johns Bluff Road, and east on Fort Caroline Road.

Fort Matanzas National Monument

c/o Castillo de San Marcos National Monument
1 Castillo Drive South
St. Augustine, FL 32084-3699
904-471-0116

This 227-acre national monument on Florida's northeast coast protects and interprets the place where, in 1565 Spanish soldiers from St. Augustine slaughtered (*matanzas* in Spanish) nearly 250 Frenchmen from Fort Caroline, whose fleet of warships had been shipwrecked by a hurricane. The French military forces had been preparing to attack St. Augustine and seize control of this region of North America. Next, however, Britain challenged Spain's claim to the region when, in 1740 British forces blockaded the Matanzas River and prepared to attack St. Augustine and its massive fort. After a brief engagement at the mouth of Matanzas Inlet, Spanish supply ships succeeded in slipping past the blockade to deliver urgently needed provisions to St. Augustine, and five weeks after initiating the blockade, the British ended their plan to attack St. Augustine. As a consequence of the threat from Britain, the Spaniards then built a small but sturdy stone fort at the mouth of Matanzas Inlet. It is this structure that is the highlight of the national monument.

The visitor center provides interpretive exhibits, programs, and publications. The monument is open daily, except Christmas. Access from St. Augustine is 14 miles south on State Route A1A on Anastasia Island. The fort is reached by a free ferry service, which is operated daily except when the weather does not allow safe passage.

Gulf Islands National Seashore

1801 Gulf Breeze Parkway
Gulf Breeze, FL 32561-5000
904-934-2600

This 135,607-acre national seashore, reaching 150 miles from Santa Rosa Island in Florida to West Ship Island in Mississippi, protects a

series of barrier islands in the Gulf of Mexico and other areas on the mainland. The rich cultural and natural history of the islands includes old forts, a pioneering experimental tree farm, archaeological traces of the earliest inhabitants, and a variety of flora and fauna. One of the major seashore units is the 1,300-acre Naval Live Oaks area, the name of which comes from the 18th and early 19th centuries when the wood of live oaks was prized for its strength and durability in the construction of sailing ships. The federal government acquired the oaks area in 1828 and established a federal tree farm that was the first public program by the U.S. government to conserve natural resources—a forerunner of the national forests.

Growing with the venerable Spanish moss-draped live oaks are such other trees as slash, longleaf, and sand pines, along with eastern red cedar, southern magnolia, pignut hickory, and wax myrtle. Interior sandhills support such species as pines, turkey oaks, the shrubby palmetto, and a holly known as "yaupon." Expanses of saltmarsh also border the area. Among wildlife of the seashore are raccoon, opossum, armadillo, alligator, and more than 280 species of birds, including brown pelican, a number of herons, waterfowl, shorebirds, gulls, terns, black skimmer, red-bellied woodpecker, blue jay, Carolina chickadee, tufted titmouse, brown-headed nuthatch, Carolina and marsh wrens, catbird, mockingbird, brown thrasher, cardinal, red-winged blackbird, and many species of warblers. The National Park Service cautions visitors to be alert for diamondback rattlesnakes, coral snakes, ticks, chiggers, and poison ivy. Hiking trails, the seashore's headquarters, and a visitor center providing interpretive exhibits, programs, and publications are located in this unit on Santa Rosa Peninsula. It is accessed from Pensacola on U.S. Route 98 across the Pensacola Bay Bridge.

Other seashore units in Florida protect and interpret two forts. Fort Pickens at the western end of Santa Rosa Island was built in the early 1830s to help protect the island and the strategic entrance to Pensacola Harbor. Fort Barrancas on the Pensacola Naval Air Station was built in the early 1840s to increase the harbor defenses. Visitor information stations are located near both forts. Access to

Santa Rosa Island is by way of the Pensacola Bay Bridge and another bridge from Santa Rosa Peninsula to the island; access to the Pensacola Naval Air Station is by way of State Route 295 and following signs to Fort Barrancas.

The Mississippi units of the seashore protect three sites. First, at the Davis Bayou Area on the mainland, a visitor center provides interpretive information and interpreter-guided excursions on waterways in the bayou. Second, West Ship Island is a virtually pristine barrier island, reached by concession-operated tour boats from Biloxi (Memorial Day weekend through Labor Day) and from Gulfport (March through October). And third, on West Ship Island is the 19th-century Fort Massachusetts, which was built to help protect New Orleans and the adjacent Gulf Coast. In 1862, this fort became a major staging area for the capture of New Orleans by Union forces in the Civil War.

At all these protected areas, swimmers and waders are urged to be careful of the surf. Campgrounds are located at the Fort Pickens and Davis Bayou units; for campsite reservations, contact the National Park Reservation Service at 800-365-CAMP. A campground store with food and supplies is located near Fort Pickens Campground. Primitive camping is also allowed on East Ship, Horn, and Petit Bois islands, and short-order food services are seasonally available at the Santa Rosa, Fort Pickens, and Okaloosa units and on Perdido Key and West Ship Island.

Timucuan Ecological and Historic Preserve

13165 Mt. Pleasant Road
Jacksonville, FL 32225-1227
904-641-7155

This 46,000-acre ecological and historic preserve protects and interprets an area once occupied by the Timucuan Indians, who may have been here for as long as 2,000 years. (The name "Timucuan" is usually pronounced with the accent on the second syllable.) The preserve includes ecologically rich maritime forest, wooded wetland "islands," estuaries, tidal creeks, and salt marshes of the St. John and Nassau rivers. The area preserves the remnants of Spanish, French, and English colonial sites and historic structures and grounds of the American period. A large number of slaves from Africa also lived in the Timucuan area, contributing as well to the area's cultural mix.

The flora and fauna are also diverse. Mammals include bobcat, raccoon, armadillo, marsh rabbit, river otter, gray squirrel, dolphin, and porpoise. Of the many species of birds, there are brown pelican, herons, snowy and great egrets, wood stork, numerous waterfowl, bald eagle, osprey, ground dove, barred owl, belted kingfisher, pileated and red-bellied woodpeckers, blue jay, Carolina chickadee, tufted titmouse, brown-headed nuthatch, Carolina and marsh wrens, catbird, mockingbird, brown thrasher, cardinal, painted bunting, red-winged blackbird, and numerous warblers, including yellow-rumped, northern parula, palm, pine, yellowthroat, yellow-throated, prothonotary, and hooded. The green tree frog is a common amphibian. Reptiles include alligator, diamondback terrapins and gopher tortoises, fence lizard, king and indigo snakes, and cottonmouth (water mocassin) and eastern diamondback rattlesnake. Visitors are cautioned to be especially alert for the latter two snakes, as well as for ticks. Among the trees of the preserve are the dominant slash pine and water oak, along with turkey oak, pignut hickory, and southern magnolia. Spanish moss (a member of the pineapple family) and resurrection fern festoon the branches of the oaks, creating an aura of mystery to the woodlands. Shrubs include beautyberry, yaupon, and azalea. Showy orchis and greenfly orchid are two of the many wildflowers.

The visitor center, located at Kingsley Plantation to the north of the St. Johns River, provides interpretive exhibits and programs, a demonstration garden, antebellum buildings, and the ruins of 25 tabby slave cabins (tabby is a building material derived from ground-up oyster shells mixed with mud). Also to the north of the river is the 400-acre Cedar Point Area, from which there is a beautiful vista of Kingsley Plantation across the Intracoastal Waterway. To the south of the river is the 600-acre Theodore Roosevelt Area, where visitors are offered weekend interpretive programs and hiking trails through maritime hammock forest to the edge of a saltmarsh. Additional interpre-

79

tive exhibits and information are provided at the main visitor center, shared with and located at Fort Caroline National Memorial, located within the preserve's Theodore Roosevelt Area. Access from downtown Jacksonville to the center is 13 miles east on State Route 10, north on either Monument Road or St. Johns Bluff Road, and east on Fort Caroline Road.

GEORGIA

Andersonville National Historic Site

Route 1, Box 800
Andersonville, GA 31711-9707
912-924-0343

This 494-acre national historic site in southwest Georgia protects and interprets the Civil War's largest and most famous Confederate prisoner-of-war camp and commemorates the sacrifices made by American prisoners in all wars. From February 1864 to April 1865, the 27-acre prison camp held approximately 45,000 Union prisoners of war. Nearly 13,000 of them died of disease, malnutrition, unsanitary conditions, exposure to weather, overcrowding, and inadequate medical attention. The site also includes Andersonville National Cemetery, with its 17,000 interments, more than a thousand of which are unidentified.

The visitor center provides interpretive exhibits, an audiovisual program, and publications. Because of its mission to interpret the overall POW story, Congress also selected this site for the recently dedicated National Prisoner of War Museum. Special living-history and other programs are presented periodically, and an audiotape tour is available for the self-guided drive through the site. Several short paths lead through parts of the area, including one that loops around the remnants of a star-shaped earthwork fortification. A picnic area is located along the road between the prison site and cemetery. Access to the site from I-75 near Henderson is 16 miles west to Montezuma on State Route 26, and ten miles southwest on State Route 49. From I-75 near Cordele, drive 35 miles west on U.S. Route 280 to Americus and then ten miles north on State Route 49.

Chattahoochee River National Recreation Area

1978 Island Ford Parkway
Atlanta, GA 30350-3400
770-399-8070

This 9,238-acre national recreation area in 16 land units scattered along a 48-mile stretch of the Chattahoochee River to the north and east of Atlanta protects areas of exceptional scenic, recreational, ecological, and historical value. Visitor activities include canoeing, boating (boat rentals are available), fishing, hiking (with 50 miles of trails), horseback riding, and birdwatching. Pre-Columbian archaeological sites, 19th-century historic sites, and a rich variety of natural habitats are among the area's attractions. Visitor contact stations, providing orientation, interpretive information, and publications, are located at the area's Island Ford and Paces Mill units. Shuttle-bus services are available between Paces Mill, Powers Island, and Johnson Ferry canoe- and boat-rental sites. For information on rentals and related services, which are available mostly from Memorial Day weekend through Labor Day, contact the Chattahoochee Outdoor Center at 770-395-6851. There are many picnic areas, but no campgrounds. The national recreation area is open daily, except Christmas. Access to the various units is by a number of routes from I-285 and I-75.

Chickamauga and Chattanooga National Military Park

P.O. Box 2128
Fort Oglethorpe, GA 30742-0128
706-866-9241

This 8,119-acre national military park in northwest Georgia and southeast Tennessee protects and interprets the Civil War battlefields of a major Confederate victory in the valley of West Chickamauga Creek, Georgia, on September 19-20, 1863, followed by a significant Union victory near Chattanooga, Tennessee, on November 23-25, 1863. Some of the fiercest and bloodiest fighting of the entire war occurred during these battles. The first encounter of the two armies, numbering 58,000 Union soldiers and 66,000 Confederates, took place in four miles of dense forest along the creek. Because it was nearly impossible to see the enemy except at close range, soldiers engaged in hand-to-hand combat. In the words of one, "The two armies came together like two wild beasts, and each fought as long as it could stand up in a knock-down and drag-out encounter." On the second day of heavy assaults, the Confederates finally drove a wedge through the middle of the Union lines, causing some Union soldiers to retreat in panic. They then forced the demoralized Union army to withdraw under the cover of darkness to Chattanooga. The Battle of Chickamauga (*Chickamauga* is a Cherokee name meaning "river of death") resulted in heavy casualties on both sides, totalling more than 16,000 Union and 18,000 Confederate soldiers.

Two months later, the Battle of Chattanooga occurred when the Union forces, then greatly revitalized by reinforcements to a total of 70,000 men, successfully stormed and seized control of the heights of Orchard Knob, Lookout Mountain, and Missionary Ridge. This assault caused the approximately 40,000 Confederates, who had been confident of holding these advantageous positions, to panic and retreat in disarray.

This largest Civil War park in the National Park System contains two major units and a number of other sites. The Chickamauga Battlefield and Point Park units both have visitor centers that provide interpretive exhibits, audiovisual programs, and publications. A seven-mile, self-guided interpretive drive (a tape tour is available at the visitor center) winds through Chickamauga Battlefield area; while the Point Park unit contains some of the area in which the Union army successfully took control of Lookout Mountain in the Battle of Chattanooga. A self-guided interpretive walking tour leads from the visitor center. The Adolph Ochs Museum near the Point Park Visitor Center provides exhibits on the Battle of Chattanooga and its role in helping end the Civil War. Hiking trails, some of which are open for horseback riding, lead throughout the park. During the summer, living-history demonstrations and other special programs are presented. The park is open daily, except Christmas. Access to the Chickamauga visitor center from I-24 at Chattanooga is south on

U.S. Route 27 (Rossville Boulevard) to just south of Fort Oglethorpe, or from I-75, drive west on Georgia Route 2 to Fort Oglethorpe, then just south on U.S. Route 27. Access to the Point Park visitor center on Lookout Mountain from downtown Chattanooga is on either Ochs or Scenic highways.

Cumberland Island National Seashore

P.O. Box 806
St. Marys, GA 31558-0806
912-882-4335

This 36,415-acre national seashore off Georgia's southeast coast protects an ecologically lush barrier island, containing miles of beautiful sandy beaches, sand dunes, interdunal meadows, saltmarsh, freshwater lakes, maritime woodlands of Spanish moss-draped live oaks, and forests of pines and hardwoods. The island, measuring 18 miles long by four miles at its widest, also contains the historical remains of two late-18th-century mansions and gardens and the chimneys of slave cabins.

The diverse habitats support a tremendous variety of wildlife. Mammals include whitetail deer, raccoon, marsh rabbit, gray squirrel, and armadillo. The most prominent reptile is the alligator. More than 300 species of birds have been recorded on this largest and southernmost island on the Georgia coast. Among them are brown pelican, herons, white ibis, wood stork, numerous waterfowl, gulls, terns, bald eagle, osprey, wild turkey, ground dove, yellow-billed cuckoo, barred and great horned owls, pileated and red-bellied woodpeckers, Carolina chickadee, tufted titmouse, brown-headed nuthatch, Carolina and marsh wrens, eastern bluebird, catbird, mockingbird, brown thrasher, many warblers, summer tanager, indigo and painted buntings, red-winged blackbird, boat-tailed grackle, and orchard oriole.

Activities include hiking, birdwatching, interpretive programs and tours, swimming, fishing, and tent camping. Reservations, issued at Sea Camp Visitor Center, are required for use of campsites at the one developed and four primitive camping areas. More than 30 miles of hiking trails lead off from the visitor center. Hikers should be alert for ticks, and swimmers are urged to be alert for hazardous conditions and for sharks that may be near shore. There are no lifeguards on the beaches. Periodic "managed hunts" are permitted on the island, at which time the seashore is closed to general visitation. Access to the seashore from I-95 is 13 miles east on Georgia Route 40 (just north of the Florida state line) to St. Marys, followed by a 45-minute ferry ride, for which reservations are required (call 912-882-4335). Visitors should be careful not to be late for the departure of the ferry ride back to the mainland.

Fort Frederica National Monument

Route 9, Box 286 C
St. Simons Island, GA 31522-9710
912-638-3639

This 241-acre national monument on St. Simons Island protects and interprets the remains of a British fort and adjacent settlement built from 1736 to 1748 under the leadership of General James E. Oglethorpe, who founded the colony of Georgia. This energetic man first established the city of Savannah, 18 miles up the Savannah River, and then selected a strategically located, coastal-island site on which to erect a fortified settlement. An earthenwork fort was built first, behind which the town was then organized. This community, initially consisting of 44 men and 72 women and children, grew to approximately 500 residents. It eventually contained many substantial Georgian-style houses constructed of wood and tabby, a concrete-like substance made from ground-up oyster shells.

The colony of Georgia, with its settlements at Savannah and Fort Frederica, was established to help promote Britain's claim to this region of North America and to challenge Spain's claim to the area from St. Augustine in Spanish Florida north to Charleston, South Carolina. In 1737, Oglethorpe sailed back to England seeking military troops and returned the following year with a 630-man regiment of British regulars. In 1740, Oglethorpe led a 2,000-man attack upon St. Augustine, but while his forces captured a small Spanish fortification at the mouth of the St. Johns River they failed to take control of massive Castillo San Marcos and St. Augustine.

In 1742, a Spanish armada under the leadership of the governor of Florida sailed north to invade the English colonies, with the goal of destroying Fort Frederica and other settlements as far north as Port Royal, South Carolina. Although outnumbered, the British troops on St. Simons Island successfully attacked one column of Spaniards and ambushed another in the Battle of Bloody Marsh, causing them to retreat to St. Augustine. This victory finally ended the Spanish threat to Georgia. Oglethorpe made one more unsuccessful attack upon Spanish Florida; but in 1743 he sailed back to England. Six years later, the military regiment was disbanded, and by 1755 Fort Frederica, which had flourished economically in its military role, was abandoned and gradually fell into ruin.

The visitor center provides interpretive exhibits, programs, and publications. Walking tours of historic points of interest are available, and living-history demonstrations are presented in summer. The monument is open daily, except Thanksgiving, Christmas, and New Year's Day. Access from Brunswick, Georgia, is east 12 miles by way of the F.J. Torras Causeway (toll) to St. Simons Island, and following signs to the monument entrance.

Fort Pulaski National Monument

P.O. Box 30757
Savannah, GA 31410-0757
912-786-5787

This 5,623-acre national monument, located on two low-lying, marshy islands at the mouth of the Savannah River, protects and interprets a massive brick fort, constructed over the years from 1829 to 1847. One of 30 U.S. coastal defensive fortifications built following the War of 1812, Fort Pulaski was built as a defense for the city of Savannah and was described as one of this country's "most spectacular harbor defense structures." The fort later came under attack during the Civil War when, on April 10-11, 1862, Union batteries of experimental rifled cannon positioned on nearby Tybee Island unleashed a 30-hour bombardment of the fort, then in Confederate hands. The siege caused extensive damage to part of this structure and brought about the fort's surrender by its Confederate defenders.

The visitor center provides interpretive exhibits, an audiovisual program, and publications. A self-guided walk leads visitors from the center, across the water-filled moat, and into the fort to view such features as the section of wall demolished by Union batteries and the commanding officer's room where the fort was officially surrendered to Union forces. Several paths and trails wind through the monument, but visitors are cautioned to be alert for the eastern diamondback rattlesnake that inhabits the area. A picnic area is available. The monument is open daily, except Christmas. Access to Fort Pulaski from Savannah is east 15 miles on U.S. Route 80.

Jimmy Carter National Historic Site

300 North Bond Street
Plains, GA 31780
912-824-4104

This 70-acre national historic site in southwest Georgia honoring Jimmy Carter, the 39th president of the United States, interprets his boyhood home, the high school he attended, the railroad station that was the 1976 Carter campaign headquarters, and the Carter family residence. The site represents the small-town, rural culture of the South that is deeply rooted in church, school, and agriculture. These elements formed a heritage that deeply influenced Carter's views about life and people and his belief in trying to resolve conflicts through negotiations and mediation. The Carter residence and boyhood home are not open to the public but may be viewed from the outside. The visitor center, located in the former railroad station, provides interpretive exhibits portraying the Carter presidency, as well as the farming and railroad history of the area. Self-guided tours of Plains are available. A picnic area is located at the Georgia welcome center. The site is open daily, except Thanksgiving, Christmas, and New Year's Day. Access to the site is by way of U.S. Route 280—44 miles west of I-75 or 17 miles east of State Route 520.

Kennesaw Mountain National Battlefield Park

900 Kennesaw Mountain Drive
Kennesaw, GA 30152
770-427-4686

This 2,884-acre national battlefield park in northwest Georgia protects and interprets the site of a brutal and bloody Civil War battle, which took place on hot and humid June 27, 1864, during the 100,000-man Union army's devastating march from Chattanooga to Atlanta. Union soldiers, under the command of Major Gen. William Tecumseh Sherman, were temporarily blocked by the 65,000-man Confederate Army of Tennessee, which was deeply entrenched on and around the steep slopes of the densely forested, double-peaked ridge known as Kennesaw Mountain. In an attempt to block Sherman's march, the Confederates, under Gen. Joseph E. Johnston, had constructed miles of defensive earthen-and-log breastworks—zigzagging across the surrounding ravines around the mountain. Their fortifications bristled with big guns and musketry.

The battle began with a thundering Union artillery siege, followed by a frontal attack by two forces of infantrymen. As the soldiers came within close range, however, Confederate forces opened fire, unleashing a bloody slaughter. The most fierce hand-to-hand combat occurred at a place along the breastworks, subsequently called the "Dead Angle." As the battle ended by midday, Union casualties totaled approximately 3,000, out of the 16,000 who took part in the battle; while Confederate casualties totaled fewer than 1,000. Following the unsuccessful frontal attack, Sherman resumed his previously successful outflanking maneuvers, ultimately enabling his army to seize Atlanta on September 2.

The visitor center provides interpretive exhibits, an audiovisual program, and publications. Living-history programs are presented during the summer. Self-guided tour drives and walks are available, including the Mountain Road, which winds from the visitor center up to the summit of the mountain. Hiking trails lead along the summit and southward to the spur called Pigeon Hill, where Confederate soldiers successfully fought off Union attacks. A spur road and trails lead farther south to Cheatham Hill, on which the battle's fiercest fighting occurred. At the southern end of the park, the Kolb's Farm log house, dating from 1836, briefly served as a Union headquarters and has been restored to its historic appearance. The park is open daily, except on Christmas and New Year's Day. To reach the park, take exit 116 on I-75 and drive four miles, following signs to the entrance. The park lies just west of Marietta and can also be reached northwest on Kennesaw Avenue, Old Route 41, and Stilesboro Road to the main entrance and visitor center; west on Whitlock Avenue (State Route 120) and northwest on Burnt Hickory Road to the Pigeon Hill area; or southwest on Powder Springs Road (State Route 360) to Kolb's Farm.

Ocmulgee National Monument

**1207 Emery Highway
Macon, GA 31201-4399
912-752-8257**

This 701-acre national monument on bluffs overlooking the Ocmulgee River in central Georgia protects and interprets the remains of a pre-Columbian Indian village, dating roughly from A.D. 900 to 1100 and once containing more than 1,000 residents. The monument contains seven large mounds, which were used for ceremonial and burial purposes by the Early Mississippian Indians—a sedentary farming culture that thrived throughout much of central and eastern North America. Prominent features include a restored ceremonial earth-lodge, 42 feet in diameter, that archaeologists believe served as a temple or council house for meetings of village leaders; the flat-topped, pyramidal Great Temple Mound, 45 feet high from a base, measuring 270 by 300 feet; and the truncated, seven-level, pyramidal Funeral Mound that is 25 feet high and 200 feet long. Excavations of the latter mound have revealed more than 100 burials, many containing copper and shell ornaments. Also protected here are the evidence of a stockaded English colonial trading post, dating from 1690, and an adjacent large village built by the Creek Indians to take advantage of commerce with English traders.

The visitor center contains an outstanding archaeological museum that provides interpretive exhibits on human habitation of this area from around 10,000 B.C. to the early 18th century, with an emphasis on the Early Missisippian village and its mound structures. Also available are an interpretive film and publications. A road leads to several points, and trails wind through the monument to a

number of the mounds and along the banks of Walnut Creek, a tributary of the Ocmulgee River. A picnic area is available near the visitor center. The monument is open daily, except Christmas and New Year's Day. Access is just east of Macon, on U.S. Route 80.

KENTUCKY

Abraham Lincoln Birthplace National Historic Site

**2995 Lincoln Farm Road
Hodgenville, KY 42748-9707
502-358-3137**

This 116-acre national historic site in the forested hills of central Kentucky protects the site where Abraham Lincoln, the 16th president of the United States, was born. An early-19th-century, one-room log cabin, housed inside a contrastingly imposing marble-and-granite, neoclassical memorial building, is probably not the original Lincoln cabin but is representative of the humble structure in which Lincoln was born on February 12, 1809. The visitor center provides interpretive exhibits, programs, and publications on Abraham Lincoln. Hiking trails lead through the historic farm area, to the enshrined cabin, to Sinking Spring that provided water for the Lincoln family, and through some of the beautiful oak-hickory forest. A picnic area is available. The site is open daily, except Thanksgiving and Christmas. Access from Hodgenville is south three miles on U.S. Route 31E/State Route 61.

Cumberland Gap National Historical Park

**P.O. Box 1848
Middlesboro, KY 40965-1848
606-248-2817**

This 20,454-acre national historical park, located in an area covering southeast Kentucky, northeast Tennessee, and the western tip of Virginia, protects and interprets a scenic part of Cumberland Mountain (a ridge of the Appalachian Mountains) and a historically significant natural pass through the mountains. For many centuries, Native Americans traveled back and forth between east and west through this narrow gap until, in 1750, a group led by Thomas Walker became the first white men to discover the passage. Hunters soon began venturing westward, seeking new sources of wildlife. Prominent among those early pioneers was marksman Daniel Boone, who traveled alone in the 1760s, exploring the uncharted wilderness beyond the Appalachians. In 1775, following the signing of a treaty officially ending many years of Indian hostilities in the region, Boone led a party of 30 companions, including his wife and children, to mark out a wilderness trail westward from Cumberland Gap in Kentucky, in which to establish a new homeland.

Hundreds and then thousands of pioneering emigrants from America's eastern seaboard were soon traveling into the new territory by way of the gap. By the close of the Revolutionary War in 1781, more than 12,000 people had crossed over to Kentucky on Boone's Wilderness Road. An even larger flood of settlers poured through the pass after Kentucky became the 15th state admitted into the Union. By 1800, at least 300,000 people had traveled through Cumberland Gap to establish new homes in the frontier beyond the mountains. Only as other routes of travel, such as canals and railroads, were extended westward did the flow of travelers through this pass begin to subside. During the Civil War, Cumberland Gap assumed strategic importance as military forces took advantage of the site. Control of the pass changed hands several times from Union control, to Confederate, and back to Union, but no significant battle was ever fought there.

The visitor center, near the beginning of Pinnacle Road, provides interpretive exhibits, programs, and publications. It is open daily, except Thanksgiving, Christmas, New Year's Day, and Martin Luther King Day. Roughly 50 miles of hiking trails lead through the park—from the short, easy, self-guided interpretive trail near the main campground (just north of U.S. Route 58, near the park's eastern entrance in Virginia), to 19-mile Ridge Trail that runs along the richly forested crest of Cumberland Mountain. Hikers are cautioned to be alert for snakes, poison ivy, poison oak, and poison sumac. Five hike-in campgrounds

(including one that is a horse camp) are located near Ridge Trail, and several picnic areas are available. Spur roads lead to trailheads along the eastern edge of the park, and a back road leads up to historic Hensley Settlement, a community of a dozen homesteads founded in 1904. Access to the park is west on U.S. Route 58 in Virginia; and northwest from Kentucky and southeast from Kentucky on U.S. Route 25E through the gap.

LOUISIANA

Cane River Creole National Historical Park and Heritage Area

P.O. Box 536
Natchitoches, LA 71458-0536
318-357-4237

This 206-acre national historical park in west central Louisiana is authorized to protect and interpret structures, sites, and landscapes associated with the development of Creole culture in urban and rural environments along the Cane River heritage area. Significant features include the Oakland Plantation, the outbuildings of Magnolia Plantation, Cane River corridor, the Natchitoches town historic district, Fort Jesup, and Cane River corridor. There are currently no National Park Service facilities, but visitors may tour plantations and other historic sites. Access is by way of the road following Cane River to the south of Natchitoches.

Jean Lafitte National Historical Park and Preserve

365 Canal Street, Suite 2400
New Orleans, LA 70130-1142
504-589-3882

This 20,020-acre four-unit national historical park and preserve in the Mississippi River Delta of southern Louisiana protects and interprets important aspects of both human and natural history. The Acadian Unit, through its three cultural centers, interprets Cajun culture and history; the Barataria Preserve offers hiking trails and canoe tours through delta forest and wetland habitats, including bald cypress swamp, bayou, freshwater marsh, and bottomland hardwood forest; the Chalmette Battlefield marks the scene of the 1815 Battle of New Orleans, the greatest land victory of the United States over Britain in the War of 1812; and the New Orleans Unit featuring the city's historic French Quarter celebrates its rich cultural history. The park is named for the mysterious Frenchman Jean Lafitte who came to the French colonial territory of Louisiana in 1802 and apparently was a French privateer and slave trader who preyed upon enemy ships.

The Acadian Cultural Center (318-232-0789), headquarters for this park unit, is at 501 Fisher Road, Lafayette, Louisiana. It provides interpretive exhibits, programs, and publications. Wetlands Acadian Cultural Center (504-448-1375) is along Bayou LaFourche and St. Mary St. in Thibodaux, Louisiana. It provides interpretive exhibits that portray the lifestyle of Acadians who lived off the swamps, marshes, bayous, and coastal waters by fishing, hunting, and trapping. Prairie Acadian Cultural Center (318-262-6862) is at Park Avenue and 3rd Street in Eunice, Louisiana. It portrays the heritage of the grasslands-based Acadians, who grazed livestock and raised crops.

The Chalmette Battlefield Unit is reached from Canal Street in New Orleans by way of N. Rampart Street that becomes St. Claude Avenue and then St. Bernard Highway (State Route 46); or from I-10's Chalmette exit, take State Route 47 (Paris Rd.) and turn right onto St. Bernard Highway (State Route 46) to the unit entrance. The visitor center (504-589-4430) provides interpretive exhibits, programs, and publications.

Barataria Preserve is reached from New Orleans, crossing the Greater New Orleans Bridge to the West Bank Expressway (U.S. Route 90), left onto Barataria Boulevard (State Route 45) and south seven miles to the unit entrance. The visitor center (504-589-2330) is at 7400 Highway 45 in Marrero, Louisiana.

The New Orleans Unit (504-589-2636) is reached south from eastbound I-10's Vieux Carre exit, then south on Basin Street, left onto Toulouse to enter the French Quarter, and left onto Decatur to enter the French Market. From westbound I-10's Vieux Carre exit, drive south on Orleans that becomes Basin Street and proceed as above.

New Orleans Jazz National Historical Park

c/o Jean Lafitte National Historical Park and Preserve
365 Canal Street, Suite 2400
New Orleans, LA 70130-1142
504-589-3882

This national historical park was established to commemorate the history of jazz, a "rare and invaluable national treasure of international importance" that is the "most widely recognized indigenous art form" in the United States, as declared by Congress in the enabling legislation. The park consists of designated sites in and around the city significant to the origins and development of the music. No properties have yet been acquired by the National Park Service, but among potential locations are Perseverance Hall, in which some of New Orlean's earliest jazz music was presented; Odd Fellows and Masonic Dance Hall-and-Eagle Saloon; Frank Early's Saloon; The Red Onion; Francis Amis Hall, a former Creole dance hall where jazz bands performed; Iroquois Theater, an African-American vaudeville center; and the Tango Belt, where the Original Dixieland Jazz Band and the New Orleans Rhythm Kings played before moving to the upper Midwest.

Poverty Point National Monument

c/o Poverty Point State Commemorative Area
P.O. Box 248
Epps, LA 71237
318-926-5492

This 910-acre national monument in northeast Louisiana focuses attention on a major pre-Columbian culture that flourished in this region more than 3,000 years ago. The culture's main physical evidence comprises what may have been the most extensive and elaborate groupings of ancient earthworks in North America, dating from around 1400 to 1350 B.C. The community was built in six concentric arcs forming a large semicircle. Each arc is an earthwork ridge measuring ten to 15 feet high and 50 to 150 feet across. A huge bird-shaped mound measuring 70 feet high and 700 feet across is connected to the outermost arc. The community became a major center for ceremonial activities and extensive trade in such items as metal artifacts and colorful stones.

The monument is presently managed by Louisiana's Office of State Parks, whose facilities are open to the public. The visitor center provides interpretive exhibits and an introductory video. From Easter to Labor Day, the park offers interpreter-guided tours by tram. Several hiking trails, including a self-guided nature trail, lead through the area. A picnic area is available. Access to the park from I-20 is ten miles north on State Route 17 to Epps, five miles east on State Route 134, and one mile north on State Route 577.

MISSISSIPPI

Brices Cross Roads National Battlefield Site

c/o Natchez Trace Parkway
2680 Natchez Trace Parkway
Tupelo, MS 38801-9718
601-680-4025

This one-acre national battlefield site in northeast Mississippi protects and interprets a small part of a Civil War battlefield, where 3,500 Confederate cavalrymen under the command of Major Gen. Nathan Bedford Forrest demonstrated outstanding tactical skill against more than 8,000 Union troops. On June 10, 1864, a hot, muggy day, the greatly outnumbered Confederates launched a fierce assault upon exhausted Union infantrymen, who had been slogging through mud to reach the area. Two hours after the Confederate army charged Union lines "with the ferocity of wild beasts," the Union soldiers became confused, panicked, and hastily retreated into Tennessee. Casualties totaled more than 2,000 Union and about 500 Confederates soldiers.

The site has no facilities, except for interpretive panels and markers. Interpretive exhibits, a film, and publications are provided at a city of Baldwin visitor center, three miles to the east, at the intersection of U.S. Route 45 and State Route 370. Access to the site from Tupelo is 14 miles north on U.S. Route 45 and several miles west on State Route 370.

Natchez National Historical Park

P.O. Box 1208
Natchez, MS 39121-1208
601-446-5790

This 108-acre national historical park protects and interprets an antebellum estate, "Melrose," that dates from 1848. This stately mansion, at 1 Melrose-Montebello Parkway, is a blend of 19th-century Greek Revival and 18th-century Georgian architectural styles, and many of the original furnishings still grace the spacious rooms. Eighty-four acres of landscaped grounds include great spreading live oaks, southern magnolias, flowering dogwoods, rhododendrons, azaleas, and a formal flower garden.

A separate unit of the park protects and interprets the William Johnson House, a brick townhouse at 210 State Street. Johnson, who was black, was born a slave in 1809, but was freed at the age of 11. He owned his own barber shop and, at age 32, built this house. He was later killed in an argument. His murderer was never apprehended.

The National Park Service offers guided tours at both units (a fee is charged at Melrose). The park is open daily, except Thanksgiving, Christmas, and New Year's Day.

Natchez Trace National Scenic Trail

c/o Natchez Trace Parkway
2680 Natchez Trace Parkway
Tupelo, MS 38801-9718
601-680-4025

Completed sections of this 694-mile trail between Nashville, Tennessee, and Natchez, Mississippi, are located along the Natchez Trace Parkway near Rocky Springs, Jackson, and Tupelo, Mississippi, and near Leipers Fork, Tennessee. Visitor activities include hiking, horseback riding, and birdwatching.

Natchez Trace Parkway

2680 Natchez Trace Parkway
Tupelo, MS 38801-9718
601-680-4025

This 51,747-acre, 424-mile-long parkway follows approximately the old Indian trace, or trail, between Nashville, Tennessee, and Natchez, Mississippi. The route is rich in Native American cultural sites and early American crafts and is the location of the Natchez Pilgrimage, which is held in the spring and fall of each year.

Tupelo National Battlefield

c/o Natchez Trace Parkway
2680 Natchez Trace Parkway
Tupelo, MS 38801-9718
601-680-4025

This one-acre national battlefield in northeast Mississippi protects and interprets a small part of the area where a Civil War battle was fought on July 14-15, 1864. More than 9,000 Confederate troops under the command of Major Gen. Nathan Bedford Forrest launched a frontal attack upon 14,000 Union forces that were dug in with entrenched fortifications along an open ridge two miles west of Tupelo. On the first day of battle, the Confederates made repeated efforts to attack union lines; but each time, Union cannon and rifle fire inflicted heavy casualties and forced the attackers to retreat. After another unsuccessful Confederate attack the following morning, the Union forces, who were suffering from the summer heat and humidity and running dangerously low on food and ammunition, decided to give up their position and withdraw northward. As they began their retreat, the Confederates began to chase the victors. Soon after, Gen. Forrest was taken out of action by a painful foot wound; however, the Confederates soon ended their pursuit. Casualties totaled more than 1,300 Confederates killed, wounded, or missing, while Union forces suffered about half that number.

The national battlefield provides a number of interpretive panels and markers. More complete interpretive information is available at the Tupelo visitor center, at milepost 266.0 on the nearby Natchez Trace Parkway. The center is open daily, except Christmas. Access to the battlefield is about one mile west of U.S. Route 45 on State Route 6.

Vicksburg National Military Park

3201 Clay Street
Vicksburg, MS 39180-3495
601-636-0583

This 1,736-acre national military park protects and interprets the Civil War site of the 47-day Union siege by Major Gen. Ulysses S. Grant's 45,000-man Army of Tennessee, culminating in the surrender of Vicksburg by its 30,000 Confederate defenders on July 4, 1863. While Grant's batteries of cannon bombarded the city and its fortifications from the land, Rear Adm. David D. Porter's ironclad naval gunboats hammered the city from the Mississippi River. Day and night, the artillery shelling rained down its destruction upon Vicksburg. Communications were severed, food and other supplies dwindled, and new supplies could not reach the city. Confederate reinforcements were blocked. And to assure the Union army's success, massive reinforcements were brought in, swelling the total to more than 70,000 soldiers.

By the end of June, Confederate soldiers were subsisting on a diet of dried beans, peas, and pea bread, supplemented by small amounts of mule meat. City residents fared even more poorly. Confederate Lieutenant Gen. John C. Pemberton, who had been under orders to defend Vicksburg, "the Gibraltar of the Confederacy," by whatever means possible, finally had no choice but to seek a negotiated surrender. Five days later, the entire length of the Mississippi River came under Union control—thereby dividing the Confederacy, with most of Texas, Arkansas, and Louisiana severed from the eight other Confederate states. Ulysses S. Grant became an instant hero in the North, lifting him ultimately to the presidency of the United States.

The visitor center provides interpretive exhibits, an audiovisual program, and publications. The 16-mile, self-guided tour drive (a tape tour is available at the center) winds through the battlefield. A series of stops highlight historically important places and events. Visitors walking in the park are urged to be alert for poison ivy and fire ants. A picnic area is available. Access to the park is by way of Clay Street (U.S. Route 80), which is reached from the West Clay Street exit from I-20. Vicksburg National Cemetery is also within the park.

Cape Lookout National Seashore

131 Charles Street
Harkers Island, NC 28531-9702
919-728-2250

This 28,243-acre national seashore protects a nearly 60-mile-long series of Atlantic coastal barrier islands along the Outer Banks of North Carolina. More remote than nearby Cape Hatteras National Seashore, Cape Lookout consists of broad beaches and low sand dunes with large areas of saltmarsh on the lagoon (inland) side of the islands. Only a few parts of the seashore support vegetation. Scattered groves of oak trees grow on Core Banks, especially at Guthrie's Hammock, while the most extensive maritime forest is on Shackleford Banks. Part of this woodland has an eerie, "ghost forest" appearance, where trees have been killed by ocean spray and shifting sands. Mammals of the seashore include river otter, raccoon, and marsh rabbit. More than 200 feral horses live on Shackleford Banks. Visitors are cautioned to keep a safe distance from these horses, as their behavior is unpredictable. Of historic interest are the U.S. Coast Guard's Cape Lookout Lighthouse at the southern end of Core Banks and Portsmouth Village, dating from 1753, at the northern end of Core Banks.

From the main visitor center on Harkers Island, passenger ferry service is offered to the southern end of Core Banks, where a small seasonally operated visitor center is located. Passenger ferry service also runs from Ocracoke, at the southern end of Cape Hatteras National Seashore, to the northern end of Core Banks, where there is a small seasonally operated visitor center and a self-guided interpretive walk through Portsmouth Village. Access to the seashore is on U.S. Route 70 to Otway and a spur road to Harkers Island.

Carl Sandburg Home National Historic Site

1928 Little River Road
Flat Rock, NC 28731-9766
704-693-4178

This 263-acre national historic site in western North Carolina honors the memory and literary accomplishments of the Pulitzer Prize-winning poet-author Carl Sandburg (1878-1967). The site protects and interprets the Sandburg farm, "Connemara," where he resided for the last 22 years of his life.

The visitor center, which occupies the ground floor of the three-story home, provides orientation, interpretive exhibits, and audiovisual programs, including an 11-minute taped interview with Sandburg in 1954 by journalist Edward R. Murrow. The center is open daily, except Christmas. The site also provides five miles of hiking trails that wind through the property, and visitors may walk around the farm to see other buildings of the farm. Access to the site is south of Ashville about 30 miles on I-26, taking exit 22 and following signs to U.S. Route 25, and left onto Little River Road.

Fort Raleigh National Historic Site

c/o Cape Hatteras National Seashore
Route 1, Box 675
Manteo, NC 27954-2708
919-473-5772

This 513-acre national historic site on Roanoke Island on North Carolina's northeast coast protects and interprets the site of England's first tentative attempts to establish a colony in North America between 1585 and 1590. After dispatching an initial reconnaissance expedition in 1584, which returned with a glowing account of the New World and its "most gentle, loving and peaceful" Indians, Queen Elizabeth I's favorite courtier, Sir Walter Raleigh, sent seven sailing ships with 107 colonists to establish an English foothold in the new land. These pioneers settled on the north end of Roanoke Island behind the barrier islands of the Outer Banks and built a small fort as a defense against attacks by French and Spanish ships. When English sailor Sir Francis Drake subsequently stopped at the settlement, he found disillusioned, starving, and homesick people, who were struggling with meager food supplies and facing increasing hostility from the Indians. Drake took them back to England. In spite of this setback, Raleigh sent another group, consisting of 84 men, 17 women, and nine children. When a ship captain returned three years later, he discovered that the little settlement and fort had been abandoned and the houses taken down. In spite of attempts between 1590 and 1602 to locate the colonists, little conclusive evidence has been found to explain what happened to the "Lost Colony."

The visitor center provides interpretive exhibits, including artifacts recovered from excavations, along with an audiovisual program and publications. At the park's Waterside Theater, *The Lost Colony* is performed during the summer, blending drama, dance, and symphonic music to convey the history of the unsuccessful attempts to colonize this part of North America. A picnic area is available. Access to the site from Manteo is three miles north on U.S. Route 64.

Guilford Courthouse National Military Park

2332 New Garden Road
Greensboro, NC 27410-2355
336-288-1776

This 220-acre national military park in north-central North Carolina protects and interprets the site of a hard-fought battle in the Revolutionary War. On March 15, 1781, American soldiers, under the command of Gen. Nathanael Greene, inflicted overwhelming losses upon British regiments before being forced to retreat in the face of a withering barrage of cannon fire, which the British aimed into the area where British and American soldiers were locked in savage combat. Only seven months after the Guilford Courthouse battle, the same British commander, Gen. Charles Earl Cornwallis, whose troops had managed to drive off the American patriots, was forced to surrender the British army to the Americans at Yorktown, Virginia, thus ending the war.

The visitor center provides interpretive exhibits, an audiovisual program, and publications. A tour road winds through the park, along which are a number of interpretive stops. Trails lead to points of interest. Among the commemorative monuments is the impressive equestrian statue of Gen. Greene. The park is open daily, except Christmas, and is

reached from U.S. Route 220 by way of New Garden Road.

Moores Creek National Battlefield

P.O. Box 69
200 Moores Creek Drive
Currie, NC 28435-0069
910-283-5591

This 86-acre national battlefield in southeast North Carolina protects and interprets the site of the Revolutionary War battle between 1,600 pro-British loyalists and 1,000 American patriots at Moores Creek Bridge on February 27, 1776. With superior artillery and musketry fire power, the American patriots wiped out virtually the entire advance unit of loyalist soldiers. Within a few minutes, the bloody encounter forced the remaining loyalists to retreat. The American victory ended British authority in the colony of North Carolina, helped to forestall a full-scale British invasion of the South, and encouraged North Carolinians to vote for independence—the first colony to do so.

The visitor center provides interpretive exhibits, an audiovisual program, and publications. Several trails loop through the area, including one that leads to the site of the history-making bridge. The reconstructed bridge is designed to suggest the appearance of the original structure and is not intended as a footbridge. Visitors are cautioned to be alert for poisonous snakes and to walk carefully near the riverbank, which may be slippery. A picnic area is available. Access to the battlefield from Wilmington is 20 miles northwest on either I-40 or U.S. Route 421, then west on State Route 210 to the entrance near Currie.

Wright Brothers National Memorial

c/o Cape Hatteras National Seashore
Route 1, Box 675
Manteo, NC 27954-2708
919-441-7430

This 428-acre national memorial on the northeast coast of North Carolina protects and interprets the place along a stretch of Atlantic Ocean beach where the first sustained flight of a heavier-than-air flying machine was achieved by Wilbur and Orville Wright on December 17, 1903. As pilot Orville Wright described the historic event: "It was the first [flight] in history in which a machine carrying a man had raised itself by its own power into the air in full flight, had sailed forward without reduction of speed, and finally landed at a point as high as that from which it started." The pioneering aircraft, *The Flyer*, had a 40-foot wingspread and a 12-horsepower engine that powered two pusher propellers. The visitor center provides interpretive exhibits, an audiovisual program, and publications. The area is open daily, except Christmas. Access to the memorial from Elizabeth City is east and south 50 miles on U.S. Route 158 to the entrance near Kill Devil Hills.

PUERTO RICO

San Juan National Historic Site

Fort San Cristobal
501 Calle Norzagaray
San Juan, Puerto Rico 00901
787-729-6960

This 75-acre national historic site in the West Indies protects and interprets the Spanish forts of *El Morro, San Cristobal*, and *El Canuelo* and the walls that encircle Old San Juan (*Viejo San Juan*). These massive masonry defenses are the oldest European-style fortifications within the territorial limits of the United States. The first significant fortification was a round stone tower, built in the late 1530s, on the rocky headland (*el morro*) at the mouth of the harbor. *Castillo de San Felipe del Morro* was gradually expanded into a massive, six-tiered sandstone fortress, with gun platforms, bastions for batteries of cannon, storerooms, gun rooms, quarters for troops, assembly court-yard, chapel, prison, dry moat, and a number of round sentry boxes attached to the outer corners of the fort. Military action experienced by this fort occurred during the Spanish-American War, when the United States attacked San Juan in 1898, resulting in Puerto Rico being ceded to the United States.

Castillo de San Cristobal, which was con-structed mostly from 1765 to 1785, is about a mile east of *El Morro* at the opposite edge of Old San Juan and is the largest Spanish fortress in the Western Hemisphere. It was built to guard the city against attack by land, a role it performed when British troops attempted to seize San Juan in 1797. This fort's cannon fired the opening shots in the Spanish-American War in Puerto Rico. *El Canuelo* is a small stone fort built at the mouth of the Bayamon River in the 1660s to help protect inland towns from attack.

El Morro and *San Cristobal* are open daily, except Christmas. Interpretive exhibits, programs, tours, and publications are provid-ed. Self-guided maps are available in both English and Spanish. The National Park Service cautions visitors to be careful when walking the fortress ramparts, stairways, ramps, and tunnels, as their surfaces are uneven and become slippery when wet. Sturdy walking shoes are recommended. *El Canuelo* is not presently open to visitors.

SOUTH CAROLINA

Charles Pinckney National Historic Site

c/o Fort Sumter National Monument
1214 Middle Street
Sullivans Island, SC 29482-9748
803-881-5516

This 28-acre national historic site in Mt. Pleasant, South Carolina, commemorates Charles Pinckney (1757-1824), who fought in the Revolutionary War and was one of the principal framers of the U.S. Constitution. He also served as a four-term governor of South Carolina, as a member of both the U.S. Congress and Senate, and as President Thomas Jefferson's minister to Spain. The site also protects part of Pinckney's Snee Farm dating from the 1820s. The visitor center pro-vides interpretive exhibits and an audiovisual program. A picnic area is available. Access to the park from I-526 is three miles east on Long Point Road.

Congaree Swamp National Monument

200 Caroline Sims Road
Hopkins, SC 29061
803-776-4396

This 22,200-acre national monument in central South Carolina protects the last significant stand of old-growth Congaree Swamp river-bottom hardwood forest, comprising around 300 varieties of flora. The lush area, which the United Nations designated a "Man and the Biosphere Reserve," is flooded by heavy rains an average of ten times per year. These floods deposit nutrient-rich sediments on the floodplain that help produce the amazing biotic diversity.

The area provides habitat for an abundance of wildlife. Among the 40 kinds of mammals are whitetail deer, raccoon, opossum, and gray squirrel. A few of the 200 species of birds are great blue heron, wood duck, barred owl, Carolina chickadee, tufted titmouse, white-breasted nuthatch, Carolina wren, summer tanager, cardinal, a great number of warblers, including prothonotary and hooded, and all eight of the woodpeckers found in the Southeast, including red-headed, red-bellied, pileated, and red-cockaded. Among the 100 varieties of trees are bald cypress, loblolly and longleaf pines, hickories, sweet gum, water tupelo, tuliptree, swamp cottonwood, cabbage palmetto, red maple, pawpaw, and the swamp chestnut, overcup, laurel, cherrybark, and Shaumard oaks.

A half-dozen well-marked trails include the ten-mile River Trail and four-mile Weston Lake Loop Trail. A marked canoeing route follows the meandering course of Cedar Creek. The National Park Service offers interpretive programs and walks. Access to the monument from Columbia is about 20 miles southeast on State Route 48.

Cowpens National Battlefield

P.O. Box 308
Chesnee, SC 29323-0308
864-461-2828

This 841-acre national battlefield in northwest South Carolina protects and interprets the site of a spectacular and decisive Revolutionary War victory of American patriot forces and frontier militiamen under the command of Brig. Gen. Daniel Morgan over a larger regiment of pro-British loyalists. On January 17, 1781, at a crucial point in the battle, the patriots were beginning a retreat in the face of intense fighting, and Gen. Morgan made the decision to quickly turn his men around and fire at the pro-British troops at virtually point-blank range. The sudden turnaround, combined with flanking maneuvers by the militia and cavalry, caught the loyalists by total surprise and forced them to turn and run.

The visitor center provides interpretive exhibits, an audiovisual program called "Daybreak at the Cowpens," and publications. A loop road winds around the perimeter of the battlefield, offering a number of interpretive stops; a self-guided interpretive trail leads visitors through some of the key battle sites. A picnic area is available. The battlefield is open daily, except Thanksgiving, Christmas, and New Year's Day. Access from I-85 at Gaffney is 11 miles northwest on State Route 11. From U.S. Route 221 at Chesnee, it is two miles east.

Fort Sumter National Monument

1214 Middle Street
Sullivans Island, SC 29482-9748
803-883-3123

This 194-acre, two-unit national monument at the mouth of Charleston Harbor protects and interprets Fort Sumter, which dates from 1828 but is best known as the place where, on April 12-13, 1861, the first military conflict of the Civil War occurred. The monument also includes Fort Moultrie, dating from 1809, where American patriots triumphed over British troops on June 28, 1776, in one of the early battles of the Revolutionary War and from which Confederate artillery unleashed an intense, two-day bombardment that pounded the Union-held Fort Sumter. Some of the 3,000 cannonballs that slammed down upon the fort were red hot and started fires in the fort. With the Confederacy's rebellion and the defeat of the Union troops at Fort Sumter, the flame of the Civil War was ignited. Four years later to the day, the American flag was raised once again in a special Fort Sumter ceremony.

Interpretive museum exhibits, an audiovisual program, a self-guided tour, and publications are provided. The national monument is open daily, except Christmas. Access to the Fort Sumter unit is by boat (fee is charged) from City Marina on Lockwood Drive in Charleston and from Patriots Point in Mt. Pleasant. For boat schedules, contact Fort

Sumter Tours, Inc., 17 Lockwood Drive, Charleston, SC 29401; 803-722-1691. Access to the Fort Moultrie unit from Charleston is on U.S. Route 17N (business route) to Mt. Pleasant; turn right onto State Route 703 at Sullivan's Island and right onto Middle Street, proceeding two miles to the entrance.

Kings Mountain National Military Park

P.O. Box 40
Kings Mountain, NC 28086-0040
864-936-7921

This 3,945-acre national military park in northwest South Carolina protects the site of a pivotal victory by American frontiersmen against pro-British loyalist troops in the Revolutionary War on October 7, 1780. In spite of the fact that the loyalists held the advantage of occupying the high ground of this 60-foot-high ridge summit, the American patriots were hidden in the thickly forested lower slopes of Kings Mountain as the loyalists unleashed a barrage of firepower from above. While the patriots were twice driven back from storming the mountaintop, they finally succeeded in reaching its heights and engaged in fierce combat, with muskets and bayonets.

As one of the frontiersmen later said, "There flashed along its summit, and around its sides, one long sulphurous blaze." A white flag of surrender was raised by the defenders of the Kings Mountain, but the patriots ignored it and continued their bloody assault for at least another hour. The pro-British soldiers were finally able to surrender and were taken captive. This decisive American victory caused the British army to delay for three months any further military initiatives in the South. The pause, in turn, gave the Americans' Continental Army valuable time to assemble a new plan of attack against the loyalists, ultimately putting the British forces on the defensive and leading to their surrender at Yorktown.

The visitor center provides interpretive exhibits, an audiovisual program, and publications. A self-guided interpretive walking tour of the battlefield is available, and a trail loops around the mountain to the summit. Visitors are cautioned that parts of this loop trail are quite steep—a fact that helps visitors grasp how challenging it was for the patriots to dis-

lodge the loyalists from their commanding position. The park also hosts two annual living-history encampments—one on the weekend nearest October 7 and the other on a weekend in May. The park is open daily, except Thanksgiving, Christmas, and New Year's Day. Access to the park from I-85 at the town of Kings Mountain, North Carolina, is ten miles on State Route 216.

Ninety Six National Historic Site

P.O. Box 496
Ninety Six, SC 29666-0496
864-543-4068

This 989-acre national historic site in western South Carolina protects and interprets the site of a key backcountry British military outpost, number Ninety Six, which was attacked by American patriots under the command of Gen. Nathanael Greene. This was the first significant land battle in the South, during the Revolutionary War. Beginning on May 22, 1781, the 1,000-man Continental Army carried out a nearly month-long siege against the fortified British outpost, while military engineers constructed a network of trenchwork that would enable the attackers to advance close to the fortifications. When the American patriots received word that substantial British reinforcements were being dispatched to Ninety Six, Gen. Greene decided to storm the fort before his men were trapped between the two British forces. On June 18, a double-pronged attack was begun, but the defenders succeeded in launching a brutal counterattack upon the patriots, resulting in heavy casualties on both sides. Two days later, the patriots withdrew to prepare for a renewed attack. The loyalists, however, burned down what had not been destroyed in the patriots' siege of their outpost and departed.

The visitor center provides interpretive exhibits, programs, and publications. A one-mile self-guided interpretive trail leads from the center to the patriots' earthwork siege lines, the sites of the loyalists' star fort, stockaded village, and the reconstructed stockade fort. The site is open daily, except Thanksgiving, Christmas, and New Year's Day. Access from the town of Ninety Six is two miles south on State Route 248.

Overmountain Victory National Historic Trail

**National Park Service
Atlanta Federal Center
1924 Building
100 Alabama Street, S.W.
Atlanta, GA 30303
404-562-3124**

This 220-mile trail commemorates the two-week trek in 1780 by 900 American patriots who crossed the mountains of North Carolina Mountains to Kings Mountain, South Carolina, to defeat the British-led milita. The trail extends from Abingdon, Virginia, to Kings Mountain, South Carolina,

The trail crosses the Appalachian National Scenic Trail and the Blue Ridge Parkway and runs through Cowpens National Battlefield, ending at Kings Mountain National Military Park. Although most of the route is now highways and roads, a 20-mile segment winds over the mountains. The route is a cooperative project among the National Park Service, U.S. Forest Service, U.S. Army Corps of Engineers, the Overmountain Victory Trail Association (c/o Sycamore Shoals State Historic Area, Elizabethton, TN 37643); and state agencies and local groups, in North Carolina, South Carolina, Tennessee, and Virginia.

TENNESSEE

Andrew Johnson National Historic Site

**P.O. Box 1088
Greenville, TN 37744-1088
423-638-3551**

This 16-acre national historic site protects and interprets the two homes and tailor's shop of Andrew Johnson, who served from 1865 to 1869 as the 17th president of the United States. In 1860, as a U.S. senator from Tennessee and in spite of being a slaveholder, Johnson denounced the secession of the Southern pro-slavery states from the Union. President Abraham Lincoln appointed Johnson as a special advisor on Southern affairs during the Civil War, and after Union troops regained much of Tennessee from Confederate control, Lincoln named him the state's military gover-

nor. Johnson next became vice-president in the Lincoln administration, and when Lincoln was assassinated, Johnson assumed the presidency. The visitor center at College and Depot streets provides interpretive exhibits, an audiovisual program, and publications. Guided tours are offered at the Homestead on Main Street, between Summer and McKee streets, which was Johnson's home during most of his years in public office.

Big South Fork National River and Recreation Area

**4564 Leatherwood Road
Oneida, TN 37841-9544
615-879-4890**

This 125,000-acre national river and recreation area in northern Tennessee and southern Kentucky protects the scenic Big Fork of the Cumberland River and its tributaries. The river flows through gorges and forested valleys. Visitor activities include rafting, canoeing, kayaking, hiking, camping, swimming, fishing, and birdwatching. More than 100 miles of trails afford opportunities to explore the area on foot or horseback. Public hunting is permitted in part of the area during the designated season. A visitor center provides orientation and interpretive services. A campground is located near the center, and rustic lodging is offered at Charit Creek Lodge. Access to the area is by various routes from I-40 and I-75.

Fort Donelson National Battlefield

**P.O. Box 434
Dover, TN 37058-0434
615-232-5706**

This 551-acre national battlefield in northwestern Tennessee protects and interprets the site of the first significant Union Army victory in the Civil War—the surrender of Fort Donelson by its 15,000 Confederate defenders. On February 12, 1862, 27,000 Union soldiers under the command of Brig. Gen. Ulysses S. Grant surrounded the landward side of this 15-acre fortification, on a bluff overlooking the Cumberland River. Two days later, a fleet of four ironclad Union naval gunboats moved into position on the river but were driven off by Confederate artillery. The following day, Gen. Grant's forces blocked an attempted Confederate escape. That night, several thousand Confederates did manage to escape upriver, but the fort, with at least 12,000 men, was forced to unconditionally and immediately surrender. Ulysses S. Grant thereupon earned the nickname "Unconditional Surrender" Grant. Combat casualties in the battle totaled around 2,800 Union soldiers and about five times that many Confederates.

The visitor center provides interpretive exhibits, an audiovisual program, and publications. A self-guided tour drive leads to a number of historic points of interest, as does a network of self-guided interpretive trails. Visitors are cautioned to be alert for poisonous snakes and poison ivy. A picnic area is available. The battlefield is open daily, except Christmas. Access to the battlefield from Clarksville is 32 miles west on U.S. Route 79. From Paris, it is 30 miles east on U.S. Route 79.

Obed Wild and Scenic River

208 N. Maiden Street
P.O. Box 429
Wartburg, TN 37887-0429
423-346-6294

This 5,121-acre wild and scenic river on the forested Cumberland Plateau of eastern Tennessee protects 45 miles of the free-flowing stretches of the Obed River and its tributaries. This scenic area features spectacular gorges with cliffs rising as high as 500 feet above the water. Visitor activities include whitewater rafting and kayaking, swimming, fishing, camping, hiking, technical rock climbing, and birdwatching. A visitor center is located in Wartburg, which is reached north from I-40 on U.S. Route 27.

Shiloh National Military Park

Route 1, Box 9
Shiloh, TN 38376-9704
901-689-5696

This 3,972-acre national military park in southwest Tennessee protects and interprets most of the battle lines of the Civil War's first major western engagement. That battle, on April 6-7, 1862, was won by the 65,000-man Union army under the command of Major Gen. Ulysses S. Grant. Confederate troops, numbering 45,000 men, had launched an overwhelming surprise attack upon unsuspecting Union forces camped at Pittsburg Landing on the west bank of the lower Tennessee River. A brutal and bloody battle raged back and forth for two days. But on the second day, the Union forces, reinforced with 25,000 fresh troops, relentlessly hammered the Confederates, steadily pushing them back across the muddy, blood-stained land, thus regaining the ground they had lost the day before and forcing the exhausted Southerners to withdraw to their base at Corinth, Mississippi. The slaughter of combat resulted in heavy casualties on both sides—13,000 Union soldiers and nearly 11,000 Confederates. Out of the bloodshed, the Union victory ultimately opened the way for Union control of the Mississippi River.

The visitor center is open daily, except Christmas. A 9.5-mile, self-guided tour drive leads visitors to numerous interpretive stops. For this tour, audiotapes and cassette players are available for rent at the center. A picnic area is available. The park also includes the Shiloh National Cemetery and the Shiloh Indian Mounds National Historical Landmark. Access to the park from Savannah is four miles west on U.S. Route 64 and six miles south on State Route 22. From Adamsville, it is four miles east on Route 64 and six miles south on Route 22.

Stones River National Battlefield

3501 Old Nashville Highway
Murfreesboro, TN 37129-3095
615-893-9501

This 708-acre national battlefield in central Tennessee protects and interprets part of the site where, from December 31, 1862, to January 2, 1863, one of the bloodiest and most brutal Civil War conflicts occurred. The major focus of fighting centered around "Round Forest," a rocky knoll topped with trees. Union cannon and infantrymen were strategically massed on this commanding position, and as hundreds of Confederates in wave after wave charged toward the hill, the Northerners unleashed a deadly blizzard of cannon balls and rifle fire. In the last hour and a half of combat, as the Confederates were finally dislodging the Union infantrymen from their high ground, Union cannon unleashed a thunderous barrage that stopped the Confederate charge, devastated their ranks, and forced the survivors to retreat. On the following day, the Southerners withdrew. In just three days of combat, casualties totaled more than 13,000 Union soldiers and 10,000 Confederates.

While the Battle of Stones River (or of Murfreesboro) was not a decisive victory for the 43,000 Union soldiers against nearly 38,000 Southerners, it caused the demoralized Confederate forces to withdraw farther from central Tennessee, ultimately enabling the Union army to invade the Deep South.

The visitor center provides interpretive exhibits, an audiovisual program, and publications. For a tour drive leading through the area, visitors may rent an audiotape and cassette player at the center. Two trails offer opportunities to walk through the battlefield area. Ranger-led walks and talks are also offered and living-history programs are presented in the summer. Visitors are cautioned to be alert for ticks and poison ivy and to remember that Stones River is not safe for swimming or wading. A picnic area is available. Stones River National Cemetery is located within the national battlefield. The battlefield is open daily, except Christmas. Access to the battlefield from Nashville is 27 miles southeast on I-24 to Exit 78B, two miles east on State Route 96, and then north on U.S. Route 41(Broad Street) to the entrance.

Trail of Tears National Historic Trail

Long Distance Trails Group Office
National Park Service
P.O. Box 728
Santa Fe, NM 87504-0728
505-988-6888

This trail marks two of the routes that were used from June 1838 to March 1839 in the forced removal of more than 16,000 Cherokee Indians from their ancestral lands in the states of Georgia, Alabama, North Carolina, and Tennessee. Thousands of Cherokee people perished along the way. The first major relocation route extended 1,226 miles by water from Chattanooga, Tennessee; down the Tennessee, Ohio, and Mississippi rivers to the Arkansas River and ended near Tahlequah, Oklahoma—a community that today serves as the Cherokee Nation's headquarters. The second relocation route extended 826 miles by land, from Chattanooga through Nashville, Tennessee, and Hopkinsville, Kentucky; crosses the Mississippi River at Cape Girardeau, Illinois, continues through Rolla and Springfield, Missouri, and ends at Tahlequah.

Interpretive programs and exhibits are presented at such places as the Cherokee National Museum in Tahlequah, the Museum of the Cherokee Indian, in Cherokee, North Carolina, and the Trail of Tears State Park, in Missouri. Automobile tour routes, from Charleston, Tennessee, to Tahlequah are marked with signs containing the official trail logo. The national historic trail is the cooperative project involving the National Park Service, other federal, state, and local governmental agencies, the Cherokee Nation, the Eastern Board of Cherokee Indians, private landowners, and private organizations, such as the Trail of Tears Association, 1100 N. University, Suite 133, Little Rock, AR 72207; 501-666-9032.

VIRGIN ISLANDS

Buck Island Reef National Monument

P.O. Box 160
Christiansted, St. Croix, VI 00821-0160
340-773-1460

This 880-acre national monument, located a mile-and-a-half off the northeast coast of the West Indian island of St. Croix, protects one of the most magnificent and ecologically significant marine gardens in the Caribbean. Buck Island measures a mile long from east to west and a third of a mile at its widest. A trail leads to its summit, affording a view of the surrounding reef and of St. Croix. The monument's main feature is a spectacular coral barrier reef surrounding the island's eastern half and the placid emerald-green lagoon that consists of a white coral sand bottom between the reef and island.

Visitors may travel along two marked snorkeling routes to view the reef, including coral grottoes, sea fans, sea whips, gorgonias, sea fans, along with elkhorn, staghorn, yellow stinging, and brain coral and a myriad of tropical fishes, including angelfish, parrotfish, butterflyfish, queen triggerfish, trunkfish, royal gramma, trumpetfish, and tang. The island contains beautiful beaches, where hawksbill and green turtles lay their eggs. Other wildlife includes nesting brown pelicans, brown boobies, frigate birds, and terns. Visitor activities include swimming, snorkeling, diving, hiking, picnicking, birdwatching, and touring the reef by glass-bottom boat. The monument is open daily. Access is by daily concession-operated charter boat excursions from Christiansted, St. Croix.

Christiansted National Historic Site

P.O. Box 160
Christiansted, St. Croix, VI 00821-0160
340-773-1460

This 27-acre national historic site on the West Indian island of St. Croix protects and interprets some of the Danish colonial history and architecture of this port town. From the mid 18th to early 19th centuries, sugar cane cultivation under the Danish West India & Guinea Company thrived, creating great economic wealth for the sugar planters and merchants. Slavery, which finally ended in 1848, had also helped make the plantations extraordinarily profitable. Many of the buildings and homes in Christiansted, the island's largest town, reflect that luxurious lifestyle.

Among the site's historic highlights are Fort Christiansvaern, an excellent example of Danish colonial fortification architecture dating from the mid-1700s; Government House, which once housed the colonial government offices; the Danish West India & Guinea Company Warehouse; the Old Danish Customs House, where the colonial government levied taxes on exports and imports and in which the site's headquarters is now located; and the Steeple Building, the island's first Danish Lutheran church, dating from 1753 and now housing the site's museum. The National Park Service suggests that visitors begin a walking tour of the site at the fort, where a small visitor center provides information and publications.

Salt River Bay National Historical Park and Ecological Preserve

c/o Christiansted National Historic Site
P.O. Box 160
Christiansted, St. Croix, VI 00821-0160
340-773-1460

This 945-acre national historical park and ecological preserve on the West Indian island of St. Croix protects outstanding pre-Columbian, historical, scenic, and ecologically significant resources. The Salt River Bay area includes archaeological evidence of the major cultural periods in the Virgin Islands, including native Caribbean settlements of three ethnic groups: the pottery-making Igneri people; the farming Taino people, who arrived in the West Indies around A.D. 600; and the Island Caribs, who arrived around 1400. A ceremonial plaza, dating from the 13th or 14th century, along with the site of an Indian village and middens (refuse dumps) are among the park's most significant archaeological features.

Explorer Christopher Columbus dropped anchor in Salt River Bay on November 14, 1493, on his second voyage to the New World on behalf of Spain. Construction of an earthen fort at Salt River Bay was begun by the British in 1641, was completed by the Dutch the following year, and was captured by the French in 1650. After the Danish West India & Guinea Company purchased St. Croix in 1733, a gun battery and customs house were built at the bay in an attempt to curtail smuggling.

The park-preserve also protects a variety of ecologically important marine and terrestrial tropical areas, including an underwater limestone canyon, coral reefs, a tidal estuary, a salt pond, stands of mangroves, a freshwater marsh, and a variety of woodland habitats. Among the more than 100 species of birds are red-billed tropicbird, brown booby, brown pelican, magnificent frigatebird, herons, great and snowy egrets, the rare West Indian whistling duck, numerous other waterfowl, osprey, clapper rail, black-necked stilt, white-crowned pigeon, common ground dove, Antillean crested hummingbird, gray kingbird, belted kingfisher, pearly-eyed thrasher, bananaquit, black-faced grassquit, and numerous warblers. There are 28 federally and locally listed endangered species of fauna and flora in the park-preserve, among which are the hawksbill and green sea turtles. Among the many varieties of tropical fishes are angelfish, butterflyfish, and sergeant majors.

NPCA and the Virgin Islands Conservation Society were instrumental in helping to build public support for establishment of the park-preserve and in helping draft the enabling legislation in Congress that resulted in the area's addition to the National Park System in 1992. The area, which is cooperatively managed by the Virgin Islands and federal governments, is open to visitors but currently has no facilities.

FRIENDS OF THE PARKS ORGANIZATIONS

Appalachian Mountain Club
(Appalachian Nat'l Scenic Trail)
65 Woodland Street
Sherborn, MA 01770
508-653-2602

Appalachian Trail Conference
P.O. Box 807
Harpers Ferry, WV 25425
304-535-6331

Battle of Shiloh Sons
(Shiloh National Military Park)
199 Carriage
Jackson, TN 38305
901-663-7391

Blue Grass Wild Water
(Obed Wild & Scenic River)
P.O. Box 4231
Lexington, KY 40544
606-623-9067

Blue Ridge Parkway Association
P.O. Box 453
Asheville, NC 28802
704-627-3419

Carolina Canoe Club
(Obed Wild & Scenic River)
P.O. Box 12932
Raleigh, NC 27605
919-967-3265

Chattanooga Civil War Roundtable
(Chickamauga & Chattanooga Nat'l Military Park)
4 Gala Drive
Fort Oglethorpe, GA 30742
706-866-9241

Chota Canoe Club
(Obed Wild & Scenic River)
P.O. Box 8270, University Station
Knoxville, TN 37996
423-986-9387

East Tennessee Whitewater Club
(Obed Wild & Scenic River)
P.O. Box 5774
Oak Ridge, TN 36730
423-483-7894

First Flight Centennial Foundation
(Wright Brothers National Memorial)
109 E. Jones, Suite 246
Raleigh, NC 27601
919-715-0209

First Flight Society
(Wright Brothers National Memorial)
P.O. Box 1903
Kittyhawk, NC 27949
919-441-4124

Florida Trail Association
P.O. Box 13708
Gainesville, FL 32604
904-378-8823

Friends of Andersonville
c/o Andersonville Nat'l Historic Site
Route 1, Box 800
Andersonville, GA 31711
912-924-0343

Foothills Parkway Association
(Great Smoky Mountains Nat'l Park)
P.O. Box 4516
Sevierville, TN 37864
423-436-1201

Friends of Canaveral
P.O. Box 1526
New Smyrna Beach, FL 32170
904-427-4094

Friends of Chickamauga & Chattanooga
P.O. Box 748
Chattanooga, TN 37401
615-629-4366

Friends of Congaree Swamp
P.O. Box 7746
Columbia, SC 29202
803-776-9105

Friends of Connemara
(Carl Sandburg Home Nat'l Historic Site)
P.O. Box 16
Flat Rock, NC 28731
704-697-2544

Friends of Kennesaw Mountain
c/o Kennesaw Mountain Nat'l Battlefield Park
900 Kennesaw Mountain Drive
Kennesaw, GA 30152
770-422-3696

Friends of Pea Ridge
14 Glenbarr Circle
Bella Vista, AR 72739
501-855-6920

Friends of the Blue Ridge Parkway
P.O. Box 20986
Roanoke, VA 24018
704-687-8722

Friends of the Everglades
7800 Red Road, Suite 215-K
Miami, FL 33143
305-669-0858

Friends of the Fordyce
& Hot Springs Nat'l Park
P.O. Box 172
Hot Springs, AR 71902
501-624-3383

Friends of the Great Smoky Mountains
204 Cherokee Trail
Seymour, TN 37865
615-428-5785

**Friends of the Stones River
National Battlefield**
P.O. Box 4092
Murfreesboro, TN 37122
615-898-2981

**Friends of the Virgin Islands
National Park**
P.O. Box 811
St. John, VI 00831
809-779-4940

Gulf Coast Environmental Defense
(Gulf Islands National Seashore)
P.O. Box 732
Gulf Breeze, FL 32562
904-476-6862

Gulf Islands Conservancy
P.O. Box 1086
Gulfport, MS 39502
601-864-3797

**Moores Creek Battleground
Association**
c/o Moores Creek National Battlefield
P.O. Box 69
Currie, NC 28435
910-283-5591

Natchez Trace Parkway Association
P.O. Drawer A
Tupelo, MS 38802
601-842-4598

Natchez Trace Trail Conference
P.O. Box 6579
Jackson, MS 39282
601-373-1447

**North Carolina Beach Buggy
Association, Inc.**
(Cape Hatteras National Seashore)
P.O. Box 940
Manteo, NC 27954
252-473-4880

**Ocmulgee Nat'l Monument
Association**
1207 Emery Highway
Macon, GA 31201
912-752-8257

Ocracoke Preservation Society, Inc.
(Cape Hatteras Nat'l Seashore)
P.O. Box 491
Ocracoke, NC 27960
252-928-7375

Old Fort Militia
(Fort Smith Nat'l Historic Site)
P.O. Box 517
Fort Smith, AR 72902
501-782-6378

**Outer Banks Community
Foundation, The**
(Cape Hatteras Nat'l Seashore)
P.O. Box 1100
Kill Devil Hills, NC 27960
252-261-8839

Overmountain Victory Trail Association

(Kings Mountain Nat'l Military Park)
1673 W. Elk Avenue
Elizabethton, TN 37643
910-921-3750

Roanoke Island Historical Association, Inc.

(Cape Hatteras Nat'l Seashore)
1409 Highway 64/264
Manteo, NC 27954
252-473-2127

St. Croix Environmental Association

(Christiansted NHS and Salt River Bay
NHP & EP)
Christiansted, St. Croix, VI 00822
809-773-1989

Smoky Mountain Hiking Club

(Great Smoky Mountains Nat'l Park)
638 Roderick
Knoxville, TN 37923
615-693-6944

Tennessee Citizens for Wilderness Planning

(Obed Wild & Scenic River)
130 Tabor Road
Oak Ridge, TN 37830
423-482-2153

Tennessee Scenic Rivers Association

(Obed Wild & Scenic River)
1809 Shackleford Road
Nashville, TN 37215
615-865-4038

Trail of Tears Association

1100 N. University, Suite 133
Little Rock, AR 72207
501-666-9032

Vicksburg Foundation for Historic Preservation

(Vicksburg Nat'l Military Park)
P.O. Box 254
Vicksburg, MS 39180
601-636-5010

Vicksburg Trails Committee

(Vicksburg Nat'l Military Park)
503 Lakeside Drive
Vicksburg, MS 39180
601-638-1382

Cooperating Associations

Civil War Trust

1225 Eye Street, NW
Washington, DC 20005
202-326-8420

Eastern National Park & Monument Association

446 N. Lane
Conshohocken, PA 19428
610-832-0555

Florida National Parks and Monuments Association

10 Parachute Key, #51
Homestead, FL 33034
305-247-1212

Fort Frederica Association

c/o Fort Frederica National Monument
Route 9, Box 286-C
St. Simons Island, GA 31522
912-638-3639

Great Smoky Mountains Natural History Association

115 Park Headquarters Road
Gatlinburg, TN 37738
423-436-7318

Kennesaw Mountain Historical Association

c/o Kennesaw Mountain Nat'l Battlefield Park
900 Kennesaw Mountain Drive
Kennesaw, GA 30152
770-422-3696

National Trust for Historic Preservation

1785 Massachusetts Avenue, NW
Washington, DC 20036
202-673-4000

Ocmulgee National Monument Association

1207 Emery Highway
Macon, GA 31201
912-752-8257

Student Conservation Association

1800 N. Kent Street
Arlington, VA 22209
703-524-2441

LOCAL COLOR

The Wildlife

"Texas" means friend.

Texas was a country before it was a state.

25 languages.

65 nationalities.

Texans believe life is too important to be dull.

The Wildflowers

The state flower is the Bluebonnet.

Over 5,000 species of wildflowers.

There's even a Wildflower Center (Thanks to Lady Bird Johnson).

Texas does not have blue grass. It just seems that way.

It's like a whole other country.®

Even the vacations are bigger in Texas. From the yarn-spinning charm of our native citizenry to hills carpeted with our native flowers, you'll find it all in Texas. It's more than you think. It's like a whole other country. For your free Texas travel guide, you can visit our web site at ▥ **www.TravelTex.com** or call us at ☎ **1-800-8888-TEX (Ext. 1290).** So give us a call, y'all.

NPCA Checks
Save Our Parks!

Every order helps preserve our country's most precious areas. Every time you order, royalties go directly to the National Parks and Conservation Association.

Return Address Labels - six scenes match your checks!

Hemp Checkbook Cover features the NPCA logo

Cotton Covers- select your favorite scene

Acadia

Everglades

Yellowstone

Arches

Smoky Mountains

Yosemite

Beautiful rotating series features the Great Smoky Mountains, Yosemite, Arches, Yellowstone, Acadia, and Everglades National Parks.

N A T I O N A L   P A R K S   C H E C K S   O R D E R   F O R M

Check Your Choice Below:	200 Singles	150 Duplicates	Total
❏ National Parks Check Series (6 designs) (NP)	❏ $15.95	❏ $17.95	$_____
❏ 240 National Parks Labels (6 designs) (NP-LB) ....Add $12.95			$_____
Checkbook Covers:			
❏ Hemp Logo Cover (HNP-UQLO)..Add $14.95			$_____
❏ Cotton Cover (CNP -UQLO)...Add $11.95			$_____

Select Scene: ❏ Acadia ❏ Everglades ❏ Yellowstone
❏ Arches ❏ Smoky Mountains ❏ Yosemite

SUBTOTAL $_____
Add 6.5% tax *for Minnesota residents only* $_____
Delivery ❏ $1.95 per item **OR** PRIORITY ❏ $3.95 per item $_____
TOTAL ENCLOSED: $_____

GD

Payment type

❏ *Check enclosed–make payable to:* Message!Products™ *No COD's*
❏ *Debit my checking account (CHECK ORDERS ONLY)* Signature_____
❏ *Charge to:* ❏ Visa ❏ Mastercard ❏ American Express ❏ Discover

Acct. No._____Exp. Date___/___ Signature_____

IMPORTANT! Include the following with this form:

❏ Voided check indicating a starting number # _____ for your new order
   (If none given we will start your order at 101)
❏ Deposit ticket from the same account
❏ Three lines of personalization for matching labels: *(see left side!)*

_____
_____
_____

❏ Daytime Telephone Number:(_____)_____
   (CONFIDENTIAL - in case of questions about your order only)

Please allow 3-5 weeks processing & delivery OR 1-3 weeks for PRIORITY delivery

To order, send complete form to:
Message!Products   or fax to:
P.O. Box 64800   1-800-790-6684
St. Paul, MN   or order online!
55164-0800   www.messagecheck.com

QUESTIONS? 1-800-243-2565